MEMOIRS

OF THE

American Philosophical Society

HELD AT PHILADELPHIA

for

PROMOTING USEFUL KNOWLEDGE

Volume IV

1935

The Ras Shamra Mythological Texts

JAMES A. MONTGOMERY

AND

ZELLIG S. HARRIS

WIPF & STOCK • Eugene, Oregon

Wipf and Stock Publishers
199 W 8th Ave, Suite 3
Eugene, OR 97401

The Ras Shamra Mythological Texts
By Montgomery, James A. and Harris, Zellig S.
ISBN 13: 978-1-60608-378-9
Publication date 01/05/2009
Previously published by The American Philosophical Society, 1935

CONTENTS

I. Preface 1

II. Location and Discovery of the Texts 5

III. Philology of the Texts 13

(1) The Alphabet 13

(2) Orthography 15

(3) Expression of Vowels 15

(4) Character of the Dialect 16

(5) The Grammar: Morphology 18

(6) Syntax 25

IV. Literary Form of the Poems 29

V. Synopsis of the Poems 33

VI. Bibliography 43

VII. The Texts in Transcription 49

Poem A 49

Poem B 58

Poem C 75

Poem D 78

VIII. Glossary 85

IX. Supplement: Poem E with Vocabulary 131

I

PREFACE

The following is planned to be a handbook on the principal cuneiform Hebraic texts found, all in the past six years, at Ras Shamra on the North-Syrian coast. These constitute a portentous constellation in the Oriental skies, for they are to be dated in the fourteenth century B.C.E., if not earlier. The texts as published may not be generally accessible; a scholarly but scattered and often minute literature has grown up about them, which cannot easily be controlled except by specialists. In the English-speaking world not much notice has been taken of them, and public knowledge is largely confined to absurd press reports. Several eminent Hebraists have expressed the desire for such a publication, provisional as it must be. For the material presents an enormous addition to our knowledge of the philology and historical background of the Bible. As in recent years the student of the Hebrew Bible has profited from late documents like the Hebrew Ben-Sira and the Assuan papyri, with the present documents the history of the Hebrew language and of Syrian culture is pushed back toward the middle of the second pre-Christian millennium, with documents which are older than almost any which we possess in the Bible. And younger students as well should have the opportunity of delving into these texts at first hand and enjoy the vivification that must come by going outside of the Old Testament, which, with the exception of a few brief inscriptions, embraces all the older Hebrew known. Archaeology thus becomes fruitful by broadening the student's vision and counteracting the rather deadening effect of overmuch inner criticism.

Introductory sections will tell as briefly as possible of the discovery of the texts and of their epigraphy and philological interpretation. A Bibliography of the important *materialia* will inform the student where he may go for authoritative and extensive discussions. There follows a Hebrew transcription, from the original cuneiform, of the four chief documents discovered, the so-called Epical Texts. There is then given, as the most original contribution, a Glossary of the texts. The scanning of this alone will be a revelation for the contribution of those texts to the Hebrew lexicon, and even to text criticism, as many cross-references to the Bible will prove; and it may constitute for many a starting-point for farther reaches into the understanding of the civilization that lay about the early world of Israel.

This is definitely a modest undertaking; it aspires to be a means of induction into the subject for intelligent students, for whom the chief accessory textbook should be the Bible. No fresh attempts at consecutive translation are made; for the valuable experiments already presented in this line the student is referred to the several translations and commentaries listed in the Bibliography, and this as part of his discipline in a matter the science of which is still in the making. The immediate necessity is the careful study of the phonetics, the grammar, including the rather neglected syntax, and the lexicon, along with the literary form and the subject-matter of the poems, detail by detail. On these lines the following undertaking will be of value in registering the assured results of intepretation, while the queries and vacancies will honestly record the gaps in our knowledge; at the same time it is hoped that by this collection of material light will be found to have been thrown upon a number of obscure details. The present impasse of interpretation, which has followed the first brilliant and ingenious essays at translation can only yield to the method approved by the prophet Isaiah, who retorted to his opponents with their own sarcasm, "here a little and there a little."

Further similar material, as yet unpublished, has been found at Ras Shamra, including not only small tablets but also a new mythological poem. With this constant series of discoveries, and with the prospect of more, such a work as the present can only be provisional. It is also reported that inscriptions in the Phoenician alphabet have now been discovered at Byblos antedating perhaps by some centuries the notable texts recently unearthed there from the thirteenth century. The sun has dawned on an unknown and unexpected quarter, and scholarship must accordingly take new bearings.[1]

By necessity the Glossary presents only a selection of interpretations, often with question-mark, or with listing of rival suggestions, or with a sheer *non liquet*. We regret that we cannot give credit in detail to the brilliant scholars who have at large or in particular advanced the interpretation. But the volume is an introductory handbook; its main purpose is to stimulate the careful student in application to the ample but scattered discussions. For the texts presented in this volume he should in the first place avail himself of the *editiones principes* by Virolleaud in *Syria* and of the extensive treatments by Albright, Friedrich, Ginsberg. For the wider field of history of religion we would name primarily Bauer, Dussaud, Eissfeldt.

Finally, the compilers of this volume desire to express to M. Virolleaud their sense of profound obligation to him, a sentiment in which all scholarship will join. On the technical side he has published fair and faultless copies of the text. And with admir-

[1] The writers wish to express here their thanks to their colleague, Professor Speiser, who has read the manuscript and made valuable suggestions.

able and generous promptitude he has rapidly made public the rare treasures committed to his hands, while throughout this arduous work he has presented a most learned *editio princeps* of translation and interpretation of these mythological texts.

March 8, 1935.

Postscript

This volume was practically all in print, when another epical fragment appeared from M. Virolleaud's hands in *Syria*, 1935, part 1. We are fortunate in the opportunity to present it in a Supplement, and to attach to it an additional Vocabulary.

II

LOCATION AND DISCOVERY OF THE TEXTS

The texts we are concerned with were discovered at Ras Shamra, a mile inland from Minet el-Beida (the Greek Limen Leuke) to the north of L'atakia on the North-Syrian coast. The harbor of Minet el-Beida, excellent by reason of its sheltering cove, fronts Cyprus, the eastern promontory of which can be seen from the highlands above; it became naturally an entrepôt for the Mediterranean trade, both with Egypt, as is shown by Egyptian remains reaching back into the third millennium B. C., and with the Aegean "Peoples of the Sea" in the second millennium; for the latter period this westerly connection is demonstrated by abundant treasures of art and pottery, Cypriote, Cretan, Mycenaean, and notably by fine specimens of vaulted tombs of the Mycenaean style. One passage in our texts apparently refers to the well-known feathered hair-dress of the Philistines. From this thriving port the cosmopolitan trade went inland, up the Orontes valley, and striking east to the great valley of the Euphrates. The close relation of the port with inner Asia, not only with the east but also with Anatolia to the north, is proved by geographical and mythological references in the tablets, some of which are themselves in the Hurrian language, and in cuneiform texts in Akkadian and Hurrian[2]. One probable reference to Ashdod points to a close connection with the Palestinian coast and may be paralleled with Herodotus' statement of the origin of the Phoenicians from the Erythraean

[2] For the Hurrians (the Horites of the Bible) see E. A. Speiser, *Mesopotamian Origins* (1930) ch. 4, and his *Ethnic Movements in the Near East in the Second Millennium* (Offprint Series, American Oriental Society, 1933).

Sea. Egyptian influence dominated the little state in the Twelfth Dynasty, and that empire sought to cultivate with it close and friendly relations. The Mediterranean peoples then arrived, at first as traders, and later, when they were pressed out of their own lands, as marauders and conquerors, even as the Philistines conquered and settled the shore of Palestine. This exposure finally brought on the destruction of the city as a mistress of the seas; it appears to have been ruined in the thirteenth century, with only a feeble flicker of life remaining.

The little city-state, including both the port and the inland Ras Shamra, has been identified as Ugarit, known from Akkadian references; this is demonstrated by the local literary references to Ugarit, naming also the god-patron Ugar and one of its kings, Nkmd. To the north of Ugarit lies a still more distinguished point, the great promontory mountain, 1760 meters high, known to the ancients as Mons Casius, but bearing in antiquity the proud name of the Mountain of the North (Saphon). It appears to have been the domestic Olympus of the whole of Syria, and the mythology connected with it is brilliantly presented by Isaiah's caustic irony in his dirge on Assyria (chap. 14—the title naming "Babylon" must be corrected). There lived the El of the North, or simply El, as he is generally called, sometimes also known as Saphon. The cult of this Zeus-like deity was multiplied by devotion to innumerable Sons of Deity, Bne Elim, as they are constantly designated, and to a cosmopolitan group of gods and goddesses, Syrian, Babylonian, Anatolian, apparently Egyptian and Aegean, along with the deification of all the natural forces, the Baals and Asheras known in the Bible, a more abundant array than appears even in the Phoenician Sanchuniathon's listing of the local gods and mythologies. Indeed his work, preserved for us in abbreviated form by the Church Father Eusebius in his *Praeparatio evangelica*, i, 6, and the Old Testament are mutually commentaries upon one another, and equally illustrate and are illustrated by our texts.

The excavations were begun at Minet el-Beida and Ras Shamra in 1929 by the French archaeologists MM. C. F. A. Schaeffer and G. Chenet, and have been continued regularly since then. A wealth of remarkable treasures has been uncovered by these explorers, amply illustrated in the successive volumes of *Syria*, and themselves deserving tomes of publication. In the initial year, in what appeared to be a store-house, a cuneiform tablet was discovered; further investigation proved that here was a veritable scribal school and library. The stratum is of the fourteenth century. A number of diverse texts in Babylonian cuneiform was discovered, consisting of letters and the well-known syllabaries or exercises in Akkadian and Sumerian; these have been in large part published by MM. Thureau-Dangin and Virolleaud in *Syria*. But a brilliant surprise came in the discovery of a large group of tablets written indeed in cuneiform but with novel characters and in languages other than those of Babylonia.

The first lot of tablets discovered, some 48 numbers mostly fragmentary, were promptly and most commendably published by Virolleaud in *Syria* x (1929), pp. 304 ff., without translation. The problem of decipherment was immediately attacked by Professor Hans Bauer and Professor E. Dhorme; following some brief public communications the former published his attempt at decipherment in his *Entzifferung der Keilschrifttafeln von Ras Schamra*, October 1930; contemporaneously M. Dhorme's publication appeared in *Revue Biblique* xxxix (1930), pp. 571–77. By the end of that year the common labors of these two scholars had diagnosed correctly some twenty-five of the characters. Professors Virolleaud and Albright have added items, and there remain but two or three signs unknown or uncertain. See for the history of the decipherment Bauer, *Das Alphabet von Ras Schamra*

September 1932, and Albright, *Bulletin* ASOR, 46 (April 1932) p. 16.

The basis of decipherment by these first students of the texts was the general triliterality of the vocables, which were fortunately separated by small upright bars; also the number of different symbols approached the quantum of the original Semitic consonants as best preserved in the South-Semitic alphabets. As for the stimulus to the invention of a consonantal alphabet, which the Babylonians with all their science never attained, it seems reasonable to surmise that the suggestion came to the scribes of Ras Shamra from the alphabet we know as Phoenician, of which we now possess examples for the thirteenth century, while the alphabetic inscriptions from Serabit in Sinai carry back the history of that amazing invention toward the beginning of the second millennium.[3] An exact parallel to this history would be the application by the Persians in the middle of the first millennium of the cuneiform script to their alphabet. The Ugarite scribes, schooled in Babylonian styles and used to writing on clay, to which the cuneiform was peculiarly adapted, attempted an alphabet after the example of the Phoenician alphabet, perhaps in competition with it. But the ingenious labors of these scribes were doomed, either by the competition of the other far more practical alphabet, as the Persian succumbed to the Aramaic, or else by the destruction of the culture of their state by the Peoples of the Sea before their experiment had been widely accepted.[4]

This first publication of texts (to be referred to as 'T', i. e.,

[3] For the Serabit inscriptions, see Gardiner, *Jour. Eg. Arch.* 1916 p. 1, Butin, *Harv. Theol. Rev.* xxi (1928) p. 9. Cf. now also the Tell-Duweir inscription, T. H. Gaster, *Quart. Statem.* Pal. Expl. Fund 1934, 176, and E. Burrows, *ib.* 179.

[4] For the existence of various scripts in Syria cf. also the inscription from Byblos, of unknown date, written in an otherwise unknown, probably phonetic, hieroglyphic script, *Syria* 1933 (xiv) 1. Further finds in this script from Byblos (Fall, 1934) are now reported.

'Tablets') was followed in *Syria* xii (1931), pp. 193 ff., by another from the hand of Virolleaud, presenting a large clay tablet written in six columns, which the editor correctly diagnosed as a 'Phoenician Poem.' (This text will be referred to below as 'A'). Again, in *Syria* xiii (1932), pp. 112 ff., the same scholar presented a fresh text, which he entitled 'A New Song of the Poem of Alein-Baal,' on a tablet written in eight columns, four on each face. (This text will be referred to as 'B'; at the end of it, on p. 158, there is given a fragment, parallel to the end of col. vii, referred to below as 'fragm.'). Virolleaud next published a poem entitled by him 'The Birth of the Gracious and Fair Gods', in *Syria* xiv (1933), pp. 127 ff.; this text (to be referred to as 'C') consists again of one large tablet, but in a single column of wide lines. Finally, within the last half-year, the same scholar has published two fresh portions of the same series of poems. The first of these appeared in *Syria* xv (1934), pp. 226 ff.; it is a fragment of the tablet of text A, containing the beginning of column i and the end of column vi. We were fortunate in being able to include this fragment in its place before going to press. The second text appeared in *Syria* xv (1934), pp. 305 ff., and without regard to its possible logical place in the series of poems, we have been able at the last moment to enter it here as 'D'. It is these texts, mythological rather than epical, which form the immediate subject of this publication.

Virolleaud has also announced and given an abstract of a tablet which he entitles 'The Epic of Keret, King of the Sidonians' (*Revue des Études Sém.*, I, vi–xvi.); its early publication is promised.

A brief word should be said about the first group of tablets discovered and published ('T'). They are not literary texts and so have not aroused the interest their successors have enjoyed; many, too, are in fragmentary condition. For the most part they are ritual specifications of sacrifices, with calendar items, the names of a large number of deities of most cosmopolitan range, and many lists of the materialia of sacrifice. Their lexical material is therefore of great value and many of the words which can be read with certainty will be booked in the Glossary. The tablets of ritual specification are Nos. 1, 3, 5(?), 9, 12; in No. 11 the lines are all broken off except the final word which is repeated throughout, 'table', i. e. cultic table. No. 14 gives a list of temple Baals, and No. 17 a list of gods. The following are of secular character: No. 10 a list of personal names, No. 15 apparently a statement of property in a house, No. 18 a letter 'to the chief of the priests'—לרב כהנם. Several are in the Hurrian language: Nos. 4, 7, 28, 30(?), 34, 35(?) and a tablet bearing a list of gods, published in *Syria* xii (1931), p. 389. No. 2 is of especial historical interest in its listing of the Horites (Hurrians), Hittites, Subareans, Alasians (Cypriotes) and others; a recent interpretation proves it a liturgical text.

More recently, two new brief tablets were published by Dhorme in *Syria* xiv (1933), pp. 239 ff. The first of these is a religious text of 18 short lines, largely consisting of objurgations by the name of El; the second is a letter of secular order after the style of Akkadian letters, concerning some business matter which still remains obscure. The lexical material of these two texts will be listed in the Glossary, and they will be referred to as T[2] 1 or 2. Soon afterwards Virolleaud published the remains of a veterinary document, in *Syria* xv (1934), p. 75 ff. (referred to below as 'T[3]').[5] There followed an obscure tablet ('T[4]'), perhaps non-Semitic, published by Virolleaud in *Syria* xv (1934), pp. 147 ff., under the title 'Proclamation de Seleg, chef de cinq peuples', and a few tablets giving lists of names ('T[5]'), published in *Syria* xv (1934), pp. 244 ff., with the title 'Table généalogique'. Of particular interest is a tablet found by Professor E. Grant

[5] Cf. the Hittite-Mitannian text published by B. Hrozný, *Archiv Orientalní* 1931, 431–461.

at Beth Shemesh in Palestine, bearing what seems to be a docket in similar characters, written backwards. It is the first known occurrence of this script outside Ras Shamra, and was identified by Professor Albright.[6] A few such tablets are now reported from Ras Shamra itself.

In the Glossary the following points will be made: A single citation of a word or root will be given except in important or difficult cases, when several or all the citations will be given, in their context if necessary. Lexical addenda to the material in the standard Hebrew dictionaries will be presented, with such brief philological notes as may be required. Cross-reference to the Hebrew Bible will be given where mutual illumination as between the two texts can be gained; in many cases the Biblical text will be found to be approved, interpretation will often be advanced. No authorities are cited; for this reference must be made by the student to the many studies already published. Questionable readings and interpretations are marked with the interrogation point; at times various interpretations are cited. But no ample thesaurus of definitions is attempted, and the editors have had often to follow their own judgment in the mass of varying opinion.

[6] See notices by Grant and Barton, *Bulletin* ASOR, Dec. 1933, 3–6; Albright, *ib.* Feb. 1934, *Jour. Pal. Or. Soc.* 1934, 102 f.

III

THE PHILOLOGY OF THE TEXTS

(1) The Alphabet

The texts are all written on clay tablets, and in a cuneiform script, superficially similar to the Akkadian. But the combinations of wedges making up the several letters are novel and due to the inventive genius of the scribal school which produced the new alphabet. No method is apparent in the choice of signs. The writing is from left to right.

The Ras Shamra Alphabet

Sign	Hebrew		Sign	Hebrew	
𐎀	א a	See §3	𐎎	מ	m
𐎛	א̄ e	See §3	𐎐	נ	n
𐎜	א̈ u	See §3	𐎒	ס	s
𐎁	ב	b	𐎝	ס̄	s̄
𐎂	ג	g	𐎓	ע	ʿ
𐎄	ד	d	𐎔	פ	p
𐎅	ה	h	𐎕	צ	ṣ
𐎆	ו	w	𐎑	צ̄	ẓ
𐎇	ז	z	𐎖	ק	q
𐎈	ח	ḥ	𐎗	ר	r
𐎃	ח̄	ḫ	𐎌	ש	š
𐎉	ט	ṭ	𐎘	ש̄	ž
𐎊	י	y	𐎙	ת̄	ṯ
𐎋	כ	k	𐎚	ת	t
𐎍	ל	l	𐎏		X

The three alephs, which represent coloration of the laryngal by accompanying vowels, will be discussed under (3).

ד (Semitic *d* and *ḏ*) is equivalent both to Heb. ד, and to Heb. ז when = Arabic ذ, Aram. ד.

ח (Sem. *ḥ*) is Heb. ח when = Arab. ح.

ח̄ (Sem. *ḫ*) is Heb. ח when = Arab. خ.

צ̄ (Sem. *ẓ*) is Heb. צ when = Arab. ظ, Aram. ט (?).

ש is equivalent both to Heb. שׂ, and to Heb. שׁ when = Arab. س.

ת̄ (Sem. *ṯ*) is Heb. שׁ when = Arab. ث.

There are four signs the value of which is not yet certain. The sign transcribed צ̄, originally read *f*, may in some cases be actually the two signs פע as in פען, רפע. Otherwise it occurs only in a few words, as follows: חצ̄ר*, חצ̄ת, ערק̄, צ̄×י (five derivatives), צ̄ל, צ̄לל* (מצ̄לל), צ̄לם, תצ̄פן (rt. צ̄ף?), צ̄ר* (also בצ̄ר, לצ̄ר), קצ̄ב . . . . אחצ̄. In the words which are asterisked the sign may be shown to have the value *ẓ* = צ̄ (see Glossary). The virtual absence of this sign from the Tablets is to be noted.

The sign ש̊ has been taken as a mere variant of ש. But it should be a separate sign, for it occurs only in certain words, and consistently so: ש̊רת (not to be confused with בּשרת), ש̊ד (in ש̊ד אל), עש̊בת, כת×ש̊, ש̊רעה, ש̊רקם, כש̊ד; it is especially frequent in the Hurrian tablets (T 4, etc.) and occurs in the names אש̊מני and אורש̊ר. It is in general frequent in Hurrian words in the tablets and is probably a Hurrian affricate or sibilant.

The sign ס̄, accepted as a variant of ס, occurs only in the tablets, chiefly in the words כס̄א (variant of כסא 'chair'?) and ס̄ס̄ו. The sign ס occurs in other words in the same tablets.

The sign equated with × has been variously given the value of *ẓ* and *ġ*. In favor of the value *ẓ*, note the words under × in the Glossary, and מ×י, נ×ר; for the value *ġ*, see ר×ב. It must be noted, however, that *ġ* coalesces with ʿ in this dialect (e. g., בער, עלם), while *ẓ* seems to be satisfied by the sign צ̄.

(2) The Orthography

The orthography is fixed etymologically, and there are apparently no 'variant spellings' in any of the texts. In the Poems the writing is excellent, although scribal errors, confusion between similar letters, etc., naturally occur. In the Tablets, however, the writing varies: in some cases fine, in others poor, and in certain tablets the very forms do not seem to be set as yet, so that some letters are consistently written in those tablets with more wedges than they have elsewhere. The vocables are generally, almost always so in the poems, separated by a vertical stroke (cf. the separating point in the Moabite Stone). In T 37, T^2 1, T^3 A there are no such divisions; in T^2 2 the stroke is of full height with the letters.

There is variability in the handling of uniliteral elements; the conjunction ו, the interjection י, and the prepositions ב, כ, ל, may be attached to the following word or separated from it, or two such particles may be written together as one word (as in Ethiopic). In the Tablets, uniliteral words, such as ש, are attached to the preceding word. At least in one case final נ of a verbal form coalesces with the following initial נ and so is not expressed: תלך נבתם || תמטרן, i. e. *-ūn*, not *-ūna*.

(3) Expression of Vowels

All diphthongs containing *y* and *w* had become pure vowels in the speech of Ugarit, hence as in Phoenician there is no employment of ו, י for diphthongs and ultimately as matres lectionis. In לא 'not' the א must be regarded as consonantal. The final ה in the locative (שממה) and in עשרה '-teen' it is extremely difficult to explain; the ה of עשרה, points to a consonantal pronunciation at that time, for which cf. Heb. עֶשְׂרֵה-, Akk. *-ešrit.* The interrogative מה should be understood as *māhū.*

The writing is thus entirely consonantal, as it is in Phoenician. The three alephs, however, with their vocalic coloration, give us a means of diagnosing the vowel-scheme of many words, with far-reaching results. This partial representation of vowels is unique for the early history of the alphabet, which only slowly devised in various ways symbols for the vowels; it is probably due to the influence of the Babylonian system which represented the several vowels *a*, *e*, *i*, *u* by distinct signs.

Most often א, א, א represent *'a*, *'i*, *'u*: e. g. ארץ *'arṣu*, אמר *'immeru*, אגרת *'ugarit*. In forms like ישא *yissa'u* [נשא], תבא [בוא] we learn that the verbal form still retained the overhanging short vowel of the imperf. indicative. In forms like אדע 'I know', אשתינה 'I will drink it', we recognize the preformative vowel as in Hebrew. A clear distinction appears in the case-endings (see under Noun); in כסאת = *kussu'āt*, 'chairs', we have the feminine plural with the appropriate *a*–vowel.

When no vowel follows, the aleph represents the preceding vowel, thus *a'*, *i'*, *u'*: ימצא *yamṣi'*, יקרא *yiqra'*. Ginsberg, however, suggests (*JRAS* 1935, p. 45) that this is not the case, but that א is used to represent also the vowelless hamza (aleph followed by shewa).

Although the vowel was thus expressed with the aleph, the aleph itself was still felt as a definite consonant, and not once are these signs used for vowels alone; they can represent only aleph plus a vowel.

(4) Character of the Dialect

The dialect of the Semitic tablets of Ras Shamra belongs to the Hebraic stock;[7] it is an Early-Hebrew dialect. The larger alphabet (omitting the two variant alephs) is on the whole similar

[7] In the above statement 'Hebraic' is used in the broad sense which would include, e. g., Phoenician in that language stock. Others may prefer the category of 'Canaanite', so Albright, *JPOS* 1934, p. 114, n. 49. There exists a wide difference of opinion as to its place in the Semitic family. Cantineau (*Syria*, 1932) denies that it is Phoenician; his position is objected to by Dus-

to the Arabic, presenting the original richer Semitic complement of dentals, sibilants, emphatics; in the Phoenician alphabet we have a reduction of these to a simpler scale, but that is not witness against their survival in various dialects even into late times, cf. *sibboleth* and *shibboleth*. The vocabulary is in general Hebrew with the exception of what are mostly culture words of international use, these chiefly to be identified from the Akkadian, with a number demonstrably or presumably of Hurrian or Hittite origin. The inflection of the verb is, it appears, largely that of classical Hebrew, and almost all its phenomena can be paralleled in the latter. Inflectional vocalic endings in noun and verb still survived, as is indicated by the alephs, but traces of this primitive condition of nouns may be seen even in the Bible. Another important difference between the two dialects is that accented long *ā*, which became *ō* in Biblical Hebrew and Phoenician, is still *ā* here[8]: thus כסאת *kussu'āt*, *chairs*. There is here, of course, no spiration of the non-emphatic stops בגדכפת which later suffered changes in Hebrew.[9] In a word, the Hebrew student, if he controls the larger alphabet of these tablets, can read the intelligible portions with the usual apparatus of Biblical Hebrew. Many of them do not give as much trouble for interpretation as many a passage in the Bible, where of course we are dealing with a long and varied history of manuscript transmission.

saud, *Rev. Hist. Rel.* 1932, p. 274. Bauer, in his *Alphabet* calls it a 'peculiar Semitic language' and proposes for it the name 'Saphonian'; Friedrich prefers 'Ugaritic', and denies that it is either Canaanite or Aramaic, classing it under the general term 'North-West Semitic' (ZA vii, p. 311).

[8] But *ā* remained in the Babylonian pronunciation of Hebrew; cf. E. A. Speiser, The Pronunciation of Hebrew, *Jew. Quart. Rev.* xxiv (1933) 21–22.

[9] The spiration of these stops occurred at a much later date in Hebrew; cf. Bergsträsser, *Heb. Gram.* I §6m; Speiser, The Pron. of Heb., *Jew. Quart. Rev.* xvi (1926) 367 ff.

In the dialect of Ugarit the sounds *ḫ* and *ḥ*, *ṯ* and *š*, *ẓ* and *ṣ*, which have fallen together in Phoenician and Biblical Hebrew, are still distinct. In all three *ġ* has coalesced with ʻ, and *ḍ* with *ṣ*. An apparent difference of trend between this and the other Hebraic dialects occurs only in the case of Semitic *ḏ*, which coalesces with *z* in Phoenician and Biblical Hebrew, but with *d* in Ras Shamra (as in Aramaic).

Examples:

ḫ and *ḥ* distinct in RS (*ḫ*>*ḥ* in Phoen. and Heb.): אחֿד (H. אָחַז), Arab. ʼ*ḫd*, 'take'.
אחד (H. אֶחָד), Arab. ʼ*ḥd*, 'one'.

ṯ and *š* distinct in RS (*ṯ*>*š* in Ph. and H.): ת̄לת̄ (H. שָׁלֹשׁ), Arab. *ṯlṯ*, 'three'.
שמע (H. שָׁמַע), Arab. *sm*ʻ, 'hear'.

ẓ and *ṣ* distinct in RS (*ẓ*>*ṣ* in Ph. and H.): חצ̣ר (H. חָצֵר), Arab. *ḥẓr* (see Glossary).
צח (H. צָוַח), Arab. *ṣḥ*, 'cry'.

This equation depends upon the value of the sign Σ which is not quite certain.

ḏ>*d* in RS (as Aram. but >*z* in Ph. and H.): דבח (H. זבח), Arab. *ḏbḥ*, Aram. דבח, 'sacrifice'.

(5) Grammar: Morphology

The following brief notes would facilitate the reading of the texts for the Hebrew student. They assemble the principal novelties in comparison with the known Hebrew forms and constructions, call attention to the frequent survival in the latter of phenomena which characterize the former, with occasional reference to other Semitic dialects, the purpose being to articulate our dialect with its better known congeners. A rapid view of the dialectic peculiarities will enable the Hebrew student to grasp the initial difficulties. No full grammar is attempted, only in general a listing of variations from Biblical Hebrew, and with only sample forms presented. Only the forms which actually occur are given; there is no ideal reconstruction of paradigms. The citations can all be located in the text by reference to the Glossary, the roots being given where necessary. The data presented are those which are generally accepted by the scholars who have studied the text; it should be recognized that there remain many obscurities which cannot be noticed here. Grammatical references are generally made to Gesenius-Kautzsch, *Hebräische Grammatik* (GK).[10]

THE PRONOUN

1. The Personal Pronoun.

a) Absolute: Sing. I. אנך, אן; II. את; III. possibly הות (?).

b) Suffixed: Sing. I. ׳– (with verb ן–);

II. ך—; III. ה—.

Pl. I. ן— II. כם–, f. כן–;

III. הם–, ם– (m. and f.).

I Sing. In nominative no expression occurs: נפש *napši*, 'my self(?),' but ׳— with nouns in oblique cases and with plurals and duals: בת̄לחני 'at my table' (retaining primitive genitive case-ending *–i* before primitive suffix –ya), אח̄י 'my brother' (in acc. and voc.), אמי 'my mother' (voc.), בהתי (בת) (pl.), הכלי (pl.), ילדי (? dual). Plural suffix: ידן, מלכן; with impf. verb יבלנן (*–ūnanī*).

II Sing. אבך, אח̄ך; with verb ארגמך. Plural: נפשכם, with verb יעדבכם.

[10] English translation of the 25th and 28th German editions by A. E. Cowley.

III Sing. ה is written for both genders and is to be pronounced *–hū* and *–hā*. For the survival of ה = ו– in Hebrew (e. g. אהלה = אהלו) see GK §58i, §91e. With sing. noun: ראשה, עגלה, אבה (= אָבִיהוּ); with pl. בנה (= בָּנֶיהָ, בָּנָיהוּ), אחה (= אֶחָיו), אריה. With verb: תכבדה (jussive), תכבדנה (indicative); for this use of נ see below under the verb; the form with נ is the usual one in Hebrew (for cases of the former see GK §60d). Plural suffix: הם is at times written separately, as נגש הם, with verb לחם הם? (cf. עד הם, 2 Ki. 9:18). It is employed for the fem., as שפתהם (so in Heb., Ruth 1:8 ff., 22; 1 Sam. 6:7, 10). It is used with pl. nouns, as in Hebrew, e. g. ראשהם, דלתהם, שפתהם, but also with sing., e. g. פהם (פ), להם (= לָהֶם), כלהם (= 2 Sam. 23:6). But ם—seems also to occur with pl. nouns, in לפנם, and must then be explained after the Hebrew ־ֵמוֹ. With the verb ם— and הם— may be distinguished as in Hebrew, the former appearing after a final long vowel: יאחדם, תבלם (vbs. in sing.), יבלהם (vb. in pl.); cf. ם[ ]נמגנ (מגן). The following prepositional forms may be noted: בכם; לך, להם; עלך, עלם (= עָלֵימוֹ?), עלנה; בעדהם.

2. The Demonstrative-Relative ד, דת (= Arab. *ḏū*, Aram. *dī d*, Heb. זֻה, as in Gen. 31:41).

3. Interrogative מה (*māhū*), מי.

Note: For the third person m. sg. pronoun הות (?), cp. the same ת element in the Phoen. plural המת 'they', Hebrew המה. Note also the variation in these texts between המת aad הם 'there' (cp. Phoen. על and עלת).

The Noun

Simple noun-forms can generally be identified from parallelism with Hebrew and other dialects. At times the vocalic alephs attest to the vocalism: אלמן, ארבת, מאת (= מֵאָה). Transcriptions are also of avail, e. g., ידד = ιεδουδ, i. e. *yadūd*; כתר = χουσωρ (cf. כֹּשֶׁר, כּוֹשָׁרָה); חסס = Akk. *Ḫasīs*.

A few *m*–formations appear: מבך (נבך), מדד (ידד), מעצר, מפחֿם (נפחֿ); a formation in –*n* is seen in אלמן, עקלתן; with prosthetic aleph: אצבעת, ארבע (=Heb.). The occurrence here of אדן 'lord' is noteworthy.

The masc. noun normally forms the pl. in ם–: אלם, ירחֿם; similarly the dual: שמם (=–*ēm*, שָׁמַיִם) (but בנים=?). Fem. nouns end usually in –*t* and are identical in writing in sing. and pl.: מאת (sing.), מאת (pl.). They form the dual in –*tm*: תהמתם (תְּהֹם, Akk. *tiāmat*).

In the absence of vocalization, nothing can be said about the construct case except that it seems to have an analogous form to that of the Hebrew. In Aleyan, אלאין is the absolute state (אלאין בעל), and the construct is אלאי (in אלאי קרדם).

A primitive Semitic element survives in the presence of case-endings: nom. –*u*, gen. –dat. –*i*, acc. –*a* (as in Arabic, Akkadian, the Canaanite of the Amarna letters), as is witnessed by the vocalic alephs: כסא חֿבתה 'the throne (nom.) of his seat', לכסא מלכה 'to the throne of his royalty'; ליהפך כסא מלכך 'indeed he will overthrow the throne of thy royalty'; cf. also the pl. כסאת *kussu'āt*. For the survival of case-endings in Hebrew, see GK §90.[11]

The three alephs also serve to distinguish the long vowel of the pl. masc. inflection, which appears to be –*ū*, as in Arab., not –*ī*, *ē* as in Heb. Cf. the Akkadian pl. in –*ū*, and the nom. pl. in –*ū*, oblique in –*ī*, in the Hadad and Panammu (Aram.) inscrr. from Zenjirli. The abs. pl. should then be pronounced –*ūm*(*a*), cst. –*ū*, as in כסא אלם 'thrones of the gods', שנא הד 'the enemies of Haddu'.

The Heb. locative in ה appears in שממה (=שָׁמַיְמָה).

[11] For further comparative and historical material, cf. Bergsträsser, *Heb. Gram.* I §21h; Bauer and Leander, *Heb. Gram.* §65.

The Verb

The verb is rich in variety of stems. In addition to the Simple Stem (Ḳal) the following are to be listed, with cases cited that by form or syntax reveal the stem. The terminology used is that of the Hebrew paradigm.

Intensive: *Piel.* יאכל (but Ḳal תאכל), with pron. suff. תכבדנה, יכללנה.

Polel. רמם, תרממן (רום), יכננה (כון).

Pilpel. תגרגר (גור), יכרכר.

Palel. צחררת.

Quadriliteral. rt. שחוי.

Causative: *Hifil.* ימצא (with *i*–vowel), by syntax: אמלכן (note *a*–vowel of pref.), תבט (נבט).

Hofal. אמלך.

Shafel. שבער, שבעד, שקרב, שעלי (cf, GK §55i; this stem occurs only in a few words, almost all demonstrably of cultic use and merely loan-words here. It is not shown to have been a living form in this dialect).

Middle: *Nifal.* נחתא (if not Ḳal impf.); the impfs. are uncertain as such forms are mostly passives of active stems except in the series ינתכן, ינגחן, ימצחן the reciprocal meaning of which bespeak Middle form.

Ifteal. תמתחץ, אתלך (הלך) (cf. Moabite אלתחם, Biblical אֶשְׁתָּאוֹל, etc.).

Hitpael. יתעדד, תשתחוי (שחוי).

The modes of the stem are: Perfect; Imperfect with its phases Indicative, Jussive, Energetic, the Perfect and Imperfect having also Passive inflection; Imperative with its Energetic phase; Infinitive, Absolute and Construct; Participle, Active and Passive.

Perfect. Sg. 3 m.	רגם	Pl.	דבחן
f.	(?) ילת (ילד)		
2 m.	ירדת		(?) מגנתם
f.	אתות		
1.	רגמת		

The Imperf. Ind. and Juss. vary as in Arabic (also Biblical Aramaic, Early Phoenician) in that the former possesses the original overhanging vowel (*yaḳṭulu*) and bears the final epenthetic Nun after final long vowels, so that the 2 f. sg. terminates in *–īn*(*a*) and the 2 and 3 pl. in *–ūn*(*a*). For the not infrequent Hebrew parallels, see GK §47o,m. Pron. Suffixes are attached immediately to the Jussive, but to the Indicative with the intervention of the epenthetic Nun.

Imperfect. Sg. 3 m. Ind.	ישא	Pl.	ינגחן
Juss.	יקרא ; תשא		
f. Ind.	תבא		(ילד) תלדן
Juss.	תעררך		
2 m. Ind.			תמטרן
Juss.	(יתן) לתתן		
f. Ind.	תחטאן		
Juss.			
1. Ind.	אקנא'		
Juss.	אקרא		

There is also to be distinguished an Energetic in *–an* (cf. Arab. Energ. in *–an*, *–anna*): אחבן אנך ואנחן, יסתרן, יזברנן and יצמדנן (=*–ūnan*, with acc. of noun): contrast אקרא and אקראן. Outside of a few such sure cases, there arises, from the uncertain syntax and interpretation of many verbs, a problem of the character of the attached *–n*: whether it is an inflectional ending *–īn*, *–ūn*, or the Energetic, or for that matter the pronominal suffix *–n*. Moreover, a form like תעררך may represent *–ekka*< *–enka* (ךָּ‎ֶ). The Energetic form appears to be used regularly for the Indicative with pronominal suffixes. For numerous cases of this construction in Hebrew see GK §58i, §60e, Bauer and Leander, *Heb. Gram.* §48; similarly Phoenician ידברנך in the Eshmunazar insc. l. 6. Cf. also Brockelmann, *Grundriss* §259b, and South Arabic, where this augmented form had a considerable development (Hommel, *Chrest.* §38).

Passives are found in the Impf., the form being *yukṭal*: יבן בת, תעדב כסא (noun in nom.), תבלך ('be brought to thee'); for survival of the Passive Ḳal in Hebrew see GK §53u, in Amarna Canaanite see Böhl, *Sprache der Amarnabriefe* §30.

Imperative. רגם, רמם ‖ תרממן.

Infinitive. Construct (Infinitival Noun): דרע, טחן, מלך, בנשא ען.

Absolute: מאת×מא×, רא×בבת ר×ב, חכם חכמת (?).

Participle. Active, in Ḳal: עבד, נדד, pl. ינקם, הלכם.

Passive: ידד (=*yadūd*). Of Piel: מיפרת, pl. ממננם.

Weak Verbs.

פ"א: תאכל, תאחד, אאחד, יאחדם (=*yu*–, cf. Heb. variations יְאֶחֱז, יֹאחַז); יאהב; תארשן (cf. ויאצל Num. 11:25). Piel יאכל.

פ"ו: ופת: Impf. יופתן (with strong waw ?).

פ"וי: יבל: Impf. יבלנן, תבלך.

ידע: Impf. אדע.

ילד: Pf. 3 f. ילת<ילדת.

יצק: Impf. יצק.

ירד: Pf. ירדת, Impf. ירד, תרד, נרד, Impv. רד.

יתן (=Phoen. יתן, Heb. נָתַן): Pf. יתנת, Impf. תתן, Impv. תן.

also הלך: Pf. הלך, Impf. ילך, Impv. לך, Ifteal תתלכן, אתלך.

פ"ן: נבט: Impf. תבט.

נסע: Impf. יסע.

נשא: Impf. ישא (both sg. and pl.), Impv. sg. שא, pl. שא. Inf. בנשא.

נגת: Piel (?) Impf. תנגתן.

also לקח: Impf. יקח, Impv. קח.
ע"ו: בוא: Impf. תבא.
נוח: Impf. תנח.
צוח: Impf. תצח.
שית: Impf. אשת, Impv. שת.
ע"ע: סבב: Impf. נסב, Impv. סב.
נטט: Piel Impv. תנטטן.
מנן: Piel Ppl. ממננם.
ל"א: מ×מאת, מ×א, ימרא (pl.); for בוא, נשא see above.

Verbs ל"ו are strong in this dialect: מ×י, מ×ית; אחות; Piel ינאי; תכלי; תבכינה. In the Imperfect the Indicative preserves the final consonant, e. g. תכלי, but in the Jussive and Imperfect with waw consecutive the form terminates in a diphthong which has been simplified: לחשת, ויען, יעל (*ya'lē < ya'lay*, *waya'nī < waya'niy*, Cp. the noun בך 'weeping'. See ראי and נאי in the Glossary.

(6) Syntax

The difficulty of these texts lies not in their lexical material, the greater part of which by far can be recognized, but in their syntactical construction in highly dramatic and poetic compositions of novel subject-matter. The initial trouble lies in the entire absence, barring the vowel-alephs, of any representation of vowels, which constitute a major element in Semitic inflection and so are of first importance in the interpretation of the relations among the various words in a sentence.

The syntax, on the basis of present material, is that of Biblical Hebrew, with hardly an exception. The chief problem is that of the precise function of the Imperfect. A number of Perfects appear in the texts, but the Imperfect is used as the narrative tense. Only a few of these Imperfects can have futuritive force, for the poems are in themselves narrative. There is thus found a very primitive use of the Imperfect, which has its counterpart in Biblical Hebrew, especially in early poetry, and which may help to explain the features of the latter that have concerned grammarians. Waw often occurs before the Imperfect. The Perfect, on the other hand, is nominal, representing a stative condition of the verbal idea and occurring more frequently in stative verbs, e. g. שמח, מאי, אתות. A novel form of consecution of Imperfects occurs, a Jussive being followed by an Indicative: in parallelism יחבק—ישתן, B iv 13, יקרא מת בנפשה יסתרן ידר בגנגנה, B vii 47; with conjunction יקם ויופתן, B iii 13. For similar alternation between the moods of the Imperfect, cf. the South Arabic, where consecutive forms drop *-n*: Rhodokanakis, *Altsabäische Texte* I, 61. The Participle is used but rarely; absolute use of it occurs in ממנגם (see Driver, *Tenses*, p. 200). The use of the Infinitive Absolute as in South Arabic and early Syriac is also to be noted.

The direct and indirect object of a verb can both be expressed in the accusative (for Heb. cf. GK §117). The direct object, on the other hand, can be governed by ל– (see Glossary under ל) as occasionally in Heb. (generally late, GK §117n, but cases in 1 Sam. 23:10, 2 Sam. 3:30). The asseverative and vocative ל– and the ל– of purpose also occur, as also a possible enclitic particle ם– (see Glossary) which is added not only to verbs, e. g. יצקם, but also apparently to other words, e. g. גהם, דתם (ד in Glossary). Note also the particle מע suffixed to a few verbs.

The word-order is essentially as in Hebrew. The verb regularly precedes its subject, as in תתבע בתלת ענת A iv 30, passive in יבן בת לבעל B iv 62. After adverbs this order remains, thus גם יצח אל A iii 22. After certain particles, however, inversion takes place: הם יד אל מלך יחססך אהבת תר תעררך B iv 38–39, הם אמת אתרת תלבן לבנת B iv 61, אם אתתם תצחן C 39, עלן שפש תצח למת A vi 22.

The syntax of the numerals reveals an interesting phenomenon. For the ordinal a noun is used preceding the thing numbered: שבע שנת also בשבע שנת 'in the seventh year', ת̑לת̑ רבע ים 'the third, the fourth day', here with רבע as distinct from ארבע which occurs elsewhere. The form is doubtless the same as that in עָשׂוֹר 'tenth (day)' in Ex. 12:3, while the same form (*ḳaṭūl*) is used for numbering the days in Ethiopic.

An excellent example of Biblical syntax may be seen in B iii 17 ff.: [ה]ם ת̑ן דבחם שנא בעל ת̑לת̑ רכב ערפת *Lo two sacrifices hates Baal, three (hates) the Rider of the Clouds*, whereupon the three sacrifices are named. Cf. Amos 1:3 ff.

IV

THE LITERARY FORM OF THE POEMS

The literary form of these poems is that typical of Semitic verse, and its style is best exemplified by the poetry of the Bible. For the most part it is one long chain of parallel couplets, broken every now and then by a line which stands by itself. The form is simple and familiar from the Bible, as A i 11–15:

תשא גה ותצח

תשמחהת אתרת ובנה　　　אלת וצברת אריה

כמת אלאין בעל　　　כחלק זבל בעל ארץ

In point of style, a great tendency to repetition is displayed, repetition which follows from the development of the story. Thus in B v 75–103 a description of the building of Aleyan's temple is given three times. Athirat gives it in the first place and asks that it be told to Aleyan. Then Anat repeats it to him, and finally it comes in the story itself when the building begins. Similar repetitions in the course of the story occur in A ii 4–9 and 26–30, iii 2–13, iv 25–40, B i 13–19 and iv 52–57. Many phrases or scenes have become conventionalized and appear in various contexts. There is great similarity among the supplication scenes in A i 4–10, B iv 20–26, viii 26–29, and in the threat of Mot, A ii 22–25, B viii 17–24, while the terms of Anat's attack upon Mot in A ii 30–35 are recalled in Mot's challenge to Aleyan in A v 11–19. Other passages giving the central theme of some section recur of a necessity in the course of the section, and are repeated in full each time. Such is the continued recurrence of ארבת בבהתם חלן בקרב הכלם in B v, vi, vii (varied in vii to (חלן בבהתם ארבת בקרב הכלם) in the slow-moving scene of the temple window. These repetitions and set phrases give a certain Homeric touch to the literary style of the poems.

In some sections verses may be grouped together into larger divisions, each an entity in itself. Each is a unit of meaning in the poem, and each is a unit of form, in that there is a certain special interrelation among the verses of that section, beyond that which they have with the other verses. An interesting example of this is B vi 47–54, a description of a cult ceremony. Somewhat more complicated in form is B vi 22–33:

תשת אשת בבהתם
נבלאת בקרב הכלם

הן ים ות̄ן

תאכל אשת בבהתם
נבלאת בקרב הכלם

ת̄לת̄ רבע ים
תאכל . . . .

and so on for seven days. A simpler section which is nevertheless a stanza, not a mere series of parallel couplets, is found in the description of the battle of Mot and Aleyan:

יתען כגמרם   מת עז בעל עז
ינגחן כראמם   מת עז בעל עז
ינת̄כן כבת̄נם   מת עז בעל עז
ימצח̄ן כלסמם   מת קל בעל קל

The full force of the passage is seen only when these lines are taken as a single whole. In all these cases the poetic form, the arrangement of phrases, is neither arbitrary nor externally designed; it grows out of the narrative, out of its dramatic character. The result is nevertheless a formal unit which must be accepted as having an additional poetic value of its own. Such stanzas are much more frequent in poem C. A good example is C 39–49. Here there is no climactic building-up of the contents; the material itself is very simple. But the very fact that the strophic repetition does not carry the story any farther, shows that there was more here than mere interest in the story, that there was interest in the form, in the natural design of the passage. That the design was actually present is obvious from the meaning of the lines; they could be arranged only in some such way as the following (giving only the first of three almost identical verses):

נחתם ח̄טך	ימת מת	הם אח̄תם תצחן
ממנם מט ידך		
תחרר לאשת	הנל] עצר	
צחררת לפחמם		
אח̄ת אל ועלמה	אח̄ת אל	אח̄תם

The structure of the poems as a whole indicates definitely their use in liturgical recitation. The composition of the story is clearly dramatic, whence arises the strophic form noted above. It seems that at certain points the Narrator was to recite material not recorded in these texts; thus the rubric in B v 104–105 apparently refers the Narrator to some other text. Lines 1–29 of C are divided into several sections each perhaps the beginning of a poem well-known to the scribes, while in C 56–57 we have what is probably a rubric instructing the Narrator to repeat the preceding section five times.

These early liturgical forms are most instructive for our understanding of the Biblical Odes and Psalms; reference may be made to the studies of I. W. Slotki, independent of our texts, in which he seeks similar forms in the Biblical poetry.[12] For an essay at diagnosing the identical forms see Albright, *Jour. Pal. Or. Soc.* 1932, 22 f.

[12] *Jour. Bib. Lit.* 1932, 214 ff.; *Jour. Theol. Stud.* 1933, 341 ff.; *Am. Jour. Sem. Lang.* 1933–34, 15 ff.; *Journ. Manchester Eg. and Or. Society,* 1935, 31 ff.

V

SYNOPSIS OF THE POEMS

Note: The understanding of the poems will be greatly enhanced by a recognition of the structure of the various sections. The reader is urged to refer to the section on "The Literary Form", and to bear in mind the strophic arrangements in each column while reading its synopsis.

A. A Myth of the Death and Resurrection of Aleyan, God of Vegetation

In sup. i, which gives the lost beginning of col. i, the poem is entitled "To Baal" (line 1). The beginning is obscure and describes the actions of Anat (sister-consort of Aleyan) in her sorrow over Aleyan's fate (2–5), followed by her announcement that Baal (Aleyan) is dead (6). Anat suggests to Shapsh (=Shemesh, the sun-goddess) that they go down with Aleyan into the earth (7–8), and Shapsh goes down (8–9). When she is sated with weeping (9–10), Anat asks Shapsh to set (the dead) Aleyan upon her (11–12). Shapsh obeys (13); she raises Aleyan to the shoulders of Anat (14–15), that she might take him up to the Heights of the North and mourn him and bury him in a pit (15–18). Anat then slaughters as a sacrifice for Aleyan rams, sheep and other animals (18–end).

At the point where col. i first becomes intelligible (line 4) we find a goddess, probably Virgin Anat, entering the presence of El at the Source of the Rivers (4–8); she bows down before him (8–10) and announces the death of Aleyan (11–15). El then calls to Athirat (his consort) and asks her to give one of her sons that he might make him king in Aleyan's stead (15–18), but Athirat demurs (19–20). Ltpn El DPed answers (21–24), and finally she suggests that Athtar be made king in the heights of the North and sit in the throne of Aleyan (25–33). Athtar accepts (33–34), and goes to the vacated throne (35–36), ruling over the whole land of El (37).

When, after a break, the story is picked up again in col. ii, Virgin Anat is grieving (5–6) for the loss of her brother Aleyan (8–9) as an animal grieves for its young (6–8). She appeals to Mot (9–12) to bring him back, but Mot refuses (13 ff.), boasting that he will attack Aleyan, devouring him like a lamb in his mouth (21–23). Shapsh, Light of the Gods, intervenes (23–25), but as time passes (26–27) the grief of Anat continues (27–30) until finally she seizes Mot (30–31); she cleaves him with a sword (31–32), burns him in fire (33), grinds him between the mill-stones (34) and sows him in the field (34–35) that the birds may eat him (35–36).

In col. iii–iv Ltpn El DPed sees a vision in which the heavens rain oil and the streams flow with honey (4–7, repeated 10–13); it is a sign that vegetation is returning to life, and he knows thereby that Aleyan is alive (8–9, also 2–3). He is happy (14–16); he laughs and exults (16–17) that now he can rest in peace (18–19) for Aleyan is alive (20–21). El then calls Anat and instructs her to call to Shapsh (22–24), importuning her (25–27) and asking where Aleyan may be (28–29). Anat goes to her (30–32) and asks her, repeating the words of El's instructions (34–40). Shapsh then promises to seek him (41–44) while Anat asks where (45–47).

In col. v Aleyan Baal is back, smiting the powerful (1–4) and apparently trying to regain his throne (5–6). A stated time seems to pass (7–9), and Mot reappears against him (9–10) confronting him with an elaborate challenge (11 ff.).

In the beginning of col. vi Mot is set for the battle. He is with Aleyan in 12–13 (?) and is probably the speaker in 14–15.

The two fight fiercely, goring like rams, biting like serpents (16–22), until Shapsh intervenes (22–23), asking Moṫ how he dare fight with Aleyan (23–25), how he can avoid being heard by the Bull of El his father (26–27) who will then surely overturn his throne and break his kingly power (27–29). Mot goes off (30–31) and, in the broken end of the column, Aleyan apparently returns to his former position (33–35).

Sup. vi is given as a continuation of col. vi, but because of its obscurity no continuation of sense is discernible, nor is it clear how Kothar-and-Hasis enters at the last moment into the story. The last five lines are the colophon of the scribe Ilumilk (Elimelech), student (?) of the Chief of the Priests and Chief of the Shepherds (a religious title?), writing under Nkmd, king of Ugarit.

B—The Building of a Temple for Aleyan

Col. i opens with a list of the temples of various deities (13–19). After a section in which Aleyan is apparently promised the protection of Athirat (20–23) there comes an account of the casting of metal objects (for temple use, 24–30), followed by a description of the furnishings of the shrine of El (31–end).

Col. ii is very obscure, especially the beginning: something is put on the fire (8–9), then Aleyan and Anat seem to depart (13–15) while Athirat (?) asks concerning their departure (21 ff.).

In the first part of col. iii Aleyan speaks of his feasts among the Bnê Elim (? 13–16) and says that there are three sacrifices which he hates (17–18): the sacrifice of shame (18–19), the sacrifice of —— (19–20) and the sacrifice at which the women wail (for the dead vegetation god, 20–22). Aleyan and Anat come back (23–24) and apparently ask the protection of Athirat (25–26). The latter is hesitant (27–30) and refers them to El DPed (30–32), but Anat insists (32–37). Athirat seems finally to invite Anat to eat and to drink (38–40).

In col, iv–v, after an obscure section, we find Athirat coming before El (20) at the Source of the Waters (21–22); she enters and bows down (23–26). El is gracious (27–30) and inquires as to the purpose of her coming (30–32). Seeing that she is hungry (33–34), he bids her eat food and drink wine, the blood of trees, from golden cups (35–38). He assures her that his love will protect her (38–39). Athirat praises him (40–44) and then asks of him a temple for Aleyan, pointing out (50–51) that he has no shrine such as have the other gods, and listing for comparison (52–57) various temples (as in col. i). Ltpn El DPed agrees, saying that a shrine shall be built for Aleyan (58–63). Athirat praises him again (64 ff.); she describes the temple as it will be built of cedar and brick (71–73) and asks that Aleyan be given certain instructions (74–79), that he may build a temple adorned with silver and gold (80–81). Anat rejoices (82); she goes to Aleyan in the heights of the North (83–86) and brings him the good tidings (87–89), telling him that his shrine will be built (89–91) and repeating the words of Athirat's instructions (91–97, repeating 75–81). Aleyan is glad (97–98) and carries out the directions (99–102). The text is interrupted here by a rubric (104–105), perhaps instructing the Narrator to recite at this point a section from another poem. Then comes Kothar-and-Hasis, in whose hands is the building of the temple 106, (103 should probably come immediately after the rubric). A feast is prepared for him (107–108); he sits at the right of Aleyan (109–110), who describes to him the kind of temple he wants in the heights of the North (to 119). Kothar-and-Hasis suggests that a window be inserted in the shrine (120–124), but Aleyan opposes this (125–127).

In col. vi the dispute continues: Kothar-and-Hasis insists on the window (1–6) and Aleyan refuses (7–11). Kothar-and-Hasis then discusses the building (15–17). The choice cedars of Lebanon used in it are described (18–21), as is the holy (dedicatory?)

fire that burns in the new temple for seven days (22–33); silver and gold are used in the building (34–35). Aleyan rejoices (35) at this temple of silver and gold (35–38); great sacrifices of sheep and oxen are prepared (40–43) and he calls in all his fellow-gods, the "seventy sons of Athirat (Elat)" (44–46). On the several (eight?) days of the feast the gods and goddesses are alternately given (sacrificial?) animals and various cultic objects (47–54). The gods feast (55–end).

The beginning of col. vii is broken; there is some discussion entailing large numbers (of cities? 7–12). Aleyan finally agrees to the window (14–19) and Kothar-and-Hasis is now pleased to remind Aleyan that he had advised it from the first (19–28). The temple completed, Aleyan Baal is warned (?) against his enemies (35–37). He derides them, however (37–39), boasting of his might and of his rule (40–44), and defies Mot, saying that Mot shall remain in his chamber (45–49) while he, Aleyan, rules alone over the gods (49–50). The end is obscure and bears a reference to Gupn and Ugar (patrons of Byblos and Ugarit) and apparently to the Peoples of the Sea with their peculiar headdress (52–end; lines 5 ff. of the fragment constitute a better-preserved parallel to this, while 1–4 give a summary of the building of the temple).

In col. viii Aleyan is warned (by his sister Anat?) not to go to certain mountain-regions (1–8; precise sense obscure), nor to enter the city of Mot (10–15), nor yet to come near him (15–17) lest he be like a lamb in his mouth (17–20). Here Shapsh interrupts (20–26), apparently advising Aleyan to bow down before Mot (26–29) and to tell him —— (29——). The column breaks here, but the word for "my brother" remains, occurring at the end of several lines (36–38), as though Anat were anxiously calling to Aleyan. The last word in the poem is "Ugar", and a colophon along the side gives the name of Nkmd, king of Ugarit.

Note: Since this leads us directly to the battle of Aleyan and Mot, and to the death and resurrection of the former, it is quite possible that in the myths themselves the poem which is given in text A really follows this which comes in text B.

C. The Birth of the Gracious Gods

The first 29 lines are a series of short sections separated from each other by lines. They seem to contain stanzas, excerpted from various poems, to be recited by the priest in the performance of his duties. The first section (1–7) begins "I invoke the Gracious Gods" and mentions deserts (4), divine feasting (6) and Shalim, ruler of the *'rbm* and the *ṯnnm* (7); the section in 23–27 resembles this in part. The second passage (8–11) describes Mot-and-Shar, in whose hands is the scepter of barrenness and widowhood. The sections in 13–15 and in 28–29 speak of the field of Athirat-and-Raḥm and of various sacrifices, while lines 19–20 mention eight shrines of the gods. The remaining sections also contain invocations and instruction about sacrifices.

From line 30 the text is unified, containing within itself a number of stanza-like parts of various poetic forms. 31–36 is a section of unclear connotation. 37–39 is another, which deals with the lowering of the scepter of El. 39–49 contains a group of three parallel strophes (39–42, 42–46, 46–49) in which the wives of El cry out to him (calling him Mut in the first and third stanzas, Ad in the second) that his scepter is lowered and that the (sacrificial) birds are on the fire. Then comes a scene depicting the love of El and his wives (49–50), followed by an account of the birth of Shahr and Shalim (51–53): the gods are born (51–52) and the news is brought to El (52–53) who asks "To what have they given birth?" (53) and is answered "To the two children, Shahr and Shalim" (53). Instructions are given (by El?) to bring offerings to Shapsh and to the Stars (54). The scene of the love of El is then repeated (55–56) and is folowed by what appears to be a rubric instructing the Narrator to repeat this scene five times (56–57). The birth scene of 51–35 is now repeated in amplified form, except that the new-born are here called "the Gracious Gods" (58–61). After a very difficult passage, in which there seems to be mention of Ashdod, instructions are given (65) to bring offerings into the Holy Wilderness and to remain there among the stones and the trees for seven years (66), until, in the eighth season, the Gracious Gods shall reach the wilderness (67–68) where they will find the "Guardian (?) of the Sown" (68–70). The end deals with a feast of food and wine (71–end) in which the "Guardian (?) of the Sown" takes part.

D. The Death of Aleyan

Note: This poem belongs to the Aleyan group (A and B). It appeared just as the present volume was going to press, and a detailed synopsis, such as was given for the other poems, can therefore not be given here. A summary and tentative sketch is, however, appended.

In col. i someone is addressing Gupn-and-Ugar concerning his coming battle with Lotan (Leviathan) the tortuous serpent, and with the fleeting serpent (1–3), giving instructions (4), and promising to aid him and to kill his enemies (5–6), so that Mot (7–8) should have to come (as a suppliant) to Baal of the North (9–11). Gupn-and-Ugar reports (11–14) the threats of Mot (14–17). Someone else speaks (17–20) of how he shall partake of food (20–22), saying that he will eat bread and drink wine with his brethren (24–25). Lines 27–31 can be filled out completely from lines 1–5.

Col. ii begins obscurely (cf. C 61–62), mentioning the drying up of plants (5–6), a sign that all is not well with Aleyan, god of growth. Then Aleyan turns to Mot (8–11) and submits to him (11–12); he comes up to Mot (13–14) in his city (15–16); it is against this that he had been warned in B viii 10–14. Someone (Anat?) cries out (16–17) that Aleyan has submitted (17–20) repeating the words of 10–12). Mot is glad (20).

Col. iii and iv are in fragmentary condition and the progress of the story cannot be followed. There is much talk of Mot (=Yedud) in col. iii, while Baal (=Haddu) (6–7) and cups (of wine; 17–18) are mentioned in col. iv.

In col. v someone promises to place something (of Aleyan's?) in a pit (5–6; cf. A sup. i 17) and tells Aleyan to take with him (away from the upper world) (6) his clouds and wind and rain (7–8) as also his seven x (=?) and his eight (holy) swine (8–9). The gods Pdry and Tly apparently also go with him (10–11). He is warned not to enter a certain place (12–13), but to go down into the earth (14–16); for 12–16 (including the obscure 13–14) cf. the parallel passage, B viii 1–9. There follows a passage which it is difficult to connect with the preceding: Aleyan hears (17); he loves the heifer in the steppe and the cow in the field (18–21) and they bear him—(22).

In col. vi it is probably Anat who speaks (5–8; cp. A iii 19–20), announcing the death of Aleyan (=Zebul, 9–10; cp. A i 13). She turns (?) to Ltpn El DPed (11–12) who goes down and sits in mourning upon the footstool upon the ground (12–14), and pours loose earth upon his head (14–16). He performs some obscure actions as a sign of sorrow (16–22; paralleled in A sup. i 2–5) and cries (22) that Aleyan is dead (23–25; paralleled in A sup. i 6–8). He says he will go down into the earth (25), as will Anat, who will hunt for Aleyan throughout the earth (25–28; cp. A ii 15). For lines 28–31 cp. lines 5–8, 16–17 above.

Note: The close correspondence of the Aleyan poems with the themes of the Tammuz-Adonis myth must be noted here, as also the parallels to the Phoenician mythology as reported by Sanchuniathon in Eusebius' *Praeparatio*. Many obscure Biblical passages are illustrated here. For the mythological problems and patterns involved reference must be made to the extensive discussions registered in the Bibliography.

BIBLIOGRAPHY

THE EXCAVATIONS:

C. F. A. SCHAEFFER: Les Fouilles de Minet el-Beïda et de Ras Shamra, *Syria* 1929 (10) 285–297; do. (deuxième campagne). *ib.* 1931 (12) 1–14; do. (troisième campagne), *ib.* 1932 (13) 1–27; do. (quatrième campagne), *ib.* 1933 (14) 93–127; do. (cinquième campagne), *ib.* 1934 (15) 105–136. Fully illustrated articles in *Illustrated London News*, Nov. 2, 1929; Nov. 29, 1930; Nov. 21, 1931; Mar. 12, 1932; Feb. 11, 1933; Mar. 3, 1934; Feb. 16, 1935; in *L'Illustration*, Oct 12, 1929; Nov. 29, 1930; Nov. 21, 1931; Feb. 11, 1933; Mar. 3, 1934; and in *Nat. Geog. Mag.*, Oct. 1930; July 1933.

J. FRIEDRICH: Ras Schamra, ein Ueberblick ueber Funde und Forschungen, 1933, pp. 38, 8 pl. (Der Alte Orient, v. 33, pt.1/2).

ORIGINAL TEXTS:

C. VIROLLEAUD: Les inscriptions cunéiformes de Ras Shamra, *Syria* 1929 (10) 304–308, 17 pl. (T).

Un poème phénicien de Ras Shamra, *ib.* 1931 (12) 193–224, 6 pl. (A).

Vocabulaire de Ras Shamra en langue inconnue, *ib.* 1931 (12) 389–390.

Un nouveau chant du poème d'Alein Baal, *ib.* 1932 (13) 113–163, 6 pl. (B).

La naissance des dieux gracieux et beaux, *ib.* 1933 (14) 128–151. (C).

Fragments d'un traité de thérapeutique hippologique provenant de Ras Shamra, *ib.* 1934 (15) 75–83. (T^3).

Proclamation de Seleg, chef de cinq peuples, *ib.* 1934 (15) 147 ff. (T^4).

Nouveau fragment du poème de Mot et d'Aleyn-Baal, *ib.* 1934 (15) 226–243. (A sup.).

Table généalogique provenant de Ras-Shamra, *ib.* 1934 (15) 244–251. (T^5).

La mort de Baal, poème de Ras-Shamra, *ib.* 1934 (15) 305–336. (D).

E. Dhorme: Deux tablettes de Ras Shamra de la campagne de 1932, *Syria* 1933, 229–237. (T^2).

DECIPHERMENT, TRANSLATION, COMMENTARY:

W. F. ALBRIGHT: New Light on Early Canaanite Language and Literature, *Bulletin* ASOR, Apr. 1932, 15–20; More Light on the Canaanite Epic of Aleyan Baal and Mot, *ib.* Apr. 1933, 13–20; The North-Canaanite Epic of Aleyan Baal and Mot, *Jour. Pal. Or. Soc.* 1932, 185–208; The North Canaanite Poems of Aleyan Baal, *ib.* 1934, 101–140.

G. A. BARTON: A North Syrian Poem on the Conquest of Death, *Jour. Am. Or. Soc.* 1932, 221–231; A Liturgy for the Spring Festival at Jerusalem, *Jour. Bib. Lit.* 1934, 61–78; The Second Liturgical Poem from Ras Shamra, *Jour. Am. Or. Soc.* 1935, 31–58.

H. BAUER: Entzifferung der Keilschrifttafeln von Ras Schamra, Oct. 1930 (rev. by J. Friedrich, *Or. Lit.-ztg.* 1931, 714– 719). Das Alphabet von Ras Schamra 1932 (with history of decipherment, pp. 41–56 (rev. by J. Friedrich, *Or. Lit.-ztg.* 1933, 738–742).

P. (E). DHORME: Première traduction des textes phéniciens de Ras Shamra, *Rev. Bib.* 1930 (39) 571–577 (cf. p. 152), 1931 (40) 32–56. See also above under "Original Texts". (Rev. by J. Friedrich, *Or. Lit.-ztg.* 1931, 714–719.)

T. H. GASTER: A Proto-Hebrew Epic from Ras-Shamra, *Jour. Roy. As. Soc.* 1932, 857–896.

H. L. GINSBERG: Complete articles in the Hebrew journal *Tarbiṣ*, 1933 (4) 106–119, 380–390; 1934 (5) 75–90; 1935 (6) 102–105; Notes on "The Birth of the Gracious and Beautiful Gods", *Jour. Roy. As. Soc.* 1935, 45–72.

C. VIROLLEAUD: see above. Also Le déchiffrement des tablettes alphabétiques de Ras-Shamra, *Syria* 1931, 15–23; Note complémentaire sur le poème de Mot et Aleïn, *ib.* 1931, 350–357; L'épopée de Keret, *Revue des Études Sém.* I vi–xvi.

VARIA:

W. F. ALBRIGHT: A New Hebrew Literature in Cuneiform, *Jewish Forum*, March 1934; on letter of Iwir-šarri (T²), *Bulletin* ASOR 54 (April 1934), p. 26.

D. H. BANETH: Notes in *Or. Lit.-ztg.* 1932, 705; Zu dem altkan. Epos von Ras Schamra, *ib.* 449–453.

H. BAUER: Die Gottheiten von Ras Schamra, *Zts. f. d. Alttest. Wis.* 1933, 81–101; Bemerkungen zu Tafel C von Ras Schamra, *Or. Lit.-ztg.* 1934, 205; Safonisches *ib.* 1935, 129.

J. CANTINEAU: La langue de Ras Schamra, *Syria* 1932, 164–170.

E. DHORME: A propos des textes hippiatriques de Ras Shamra, *Syria* 1934, 304; La lettre d'Ewir-shar, *ib.* 1934, 395–396.

D. DIRINGER: Il nuovo alfabeto semitico di Ras Šamrah, *Biblica* 1934, 466–483.

R. DUSSAUD: Note additionelle (archaeological and historical, with map), *Syria* 1929, 297–303. Brèves remarques sur les tablettes de Ras Shamra, *Syria* 1931, 67–77. La mythologie phénicienne d'après les tablettes de Ras Shamra, *Rev. de l'Hist. d. Relig.* 1931, 353–408. Le sanctuaire et les dieux phéniciens de Ras Shamra, *ib.* 1932,

245–302. Les Phéniciens au Negeb et en Arabie d'après un texte de Ras Shamra, *ib.* 1933, 1–49, Ba'al et Ben-Dagon dans les textes de Ras Shamra, *Syria* 1934, 301-304.

E. Ebeling: Zur Entstehungsgeschichte des Keilschriftalphabets von Ras Schamra, *Sitzungsber. Berlin Akad., Phil.-Hist. Kl.* 1934, 10–15 (summarized *Zts. f. d. Alttest. Wis.* 1934, 132).

O. Eissfeldt: Baal Zaphon, Zeus Kasios und der Durchzug der Israeliten durchs Meer, 1932. Die religionsgesch. Bedeutung der Funde von Ras Schamra, *Forschungen u. Fortschritte* 1932 (8) 314 ff. Eine antike literarische Bezeugung des Ras Schamra-Alphabets (a citation from Sanchuniathon), *ib.* 1934 (10) 164–165. Die Wanderung palästinisch-syrischer Götter Ost und West, *JPOS* 1934, 294–300. Die religionsgesch. Bedeutung der Funde von Ras Schamra, *ZDMG* 1934, 173–184.

J. Friedrich: Notes in *Archiv f. Orientforschung* 1933 (8) 239–242; 1935 (10) 80. Zu den drei Aleph-Zeichen des Ras Schamra Alphabets, *Zts. f. Assyriologie* 1933 (7) 305–313. Also publication and reviews cited above.

T. H. Gaster: Ritual Pattern of a Ras Shamra Epic, *Archiv Orientalní* 1933 (5) 118–123. The Ras Shamra Texts and the Old Testament, *Quart. Statement*, Pal. Expl. Fund 1934, 141–148.

H. L. Ginsberg: Notes in *Or. Lit.-ztg.* 1933, 593–594; 1934, 473–474.

H. L. Ginsberg and B. Maisler: Semitized Hurrians in Syria and Palestine, *Jour. Pal. Or. Soc.* 1934, 243–267.

Z. S. Harris: The Structure of Ras Shamra C, *Jour. Am. Or. Soc.* 1934, 80–83; A Hurrian Affricate or Sibilant in Ras Shamra, *ib.* 1935, 95–100.

B. Hrozný: Les Ionéens à Ras Samra, *Archiv Orientalní* 1932 (4) 169–178 (cf. also *ib.* 1932, 118 ff.).

B. Maisler: Notes in *Tarbiṣ* 1933 (5) 375–380. See also above.

J. A. Montgomery: Notes on the Mythological Epic Texts from Ras Shamra, *Jour. Am. Or. Soc.* 1933, 97–123. Ras Shamra Notes II, *ib.* 1934, 60–66 (these two reprinted as Offprint No. 1 of the Journal). Additional Note, *ib.* 1933, 283–284. Ras Shamra Notes III (on Tablet 2), *ib.* 1935, 89–94. Oracle Place Names (on אלשתמעי), *JBL*, 1935, Part I.

J. P. Naish: The Ras Shamra Tablets, *Quart. Statement* Pal. Expl. Fund, 1932, 154–163.

A. T. Olmstead: Excursus on the Alphabet of Ras Shamra and its relation to the Sinaitic Inscriptions, in M. Sprengling, *The Alphabet* (Chicago 1931), 57–62.

A. H. Sayce: Etruscan Affinities in a Ras Shamra Tablet, *Jour. Roy. As. Soc.* 1932, 43–46.

C. F. A. Schaeffer: Note additionelle à propos du nom ancien de la ville Ras Sḥamra, *Syria* 1932, 24–27.

ADDENDA

R. Dussaud: Le mythe de Ba'al et d'Aleyan d'après les documents nouveaux, *Rev. de l'Hist. d. Rel.*, 1934, 5–65. Note on the Sixth Campaign, 1934, *Syria*, 1935, 110.

T. H. Gaster: The Combat of Aleyan-Baal and Mot: The Second Tablet, *Journ. R. As. Soc.* Jan. 1935.

H. L. Ginsberg: (Hebrew monograph) Epigraphical Novelties from Ugarit, *Yedi'oth* (*Bulletin*) of the Jewish Palestine Exploration Society, vol. 3, pt. 2, 1935.

W. C. Graham and H. G. May: Culture and Conscience, an Archaeological Study of the New Past in Ancient Palestine. Univ. of Chicago Press, to appear in 1935.

J. W. Jack: The Ras Shamra Tablets: Their Bearing on the Old Testament; Old Testament Studies No. 1; T. & T. Clark, 1935.

J. A. MONTGOMERY: Ras Shamra Notes IV: The Conflict of Baal and the Waters. *Jour. Am. Or. Soc.* 1935, 268–277; see Supplement to this volume.

C. F. A. SCHAEFFER: A City with Twin Temples of Dagon and Baal (report on 6th expedition, 1934), *Ill. London News*, Apr. 27, 1935, (with 28 figures).

Ç. VIROLLEAUD: La rèvolte de Košer contre Baal: Poéme de Ras Shamra, *Syria*, 1935, 29–45, (the text presented in Supplement below).

T. H. GASTER: The Chronology of Palestinian Epigraphy, *Quart. Statem.* 1935, 128–139.

W. G. Williams: The Ras Shamra Inscriptions and their Significance for the History of Religion, *Am. Journ. Sem. Lang.*, July, 1935, 233–246.

Part 2 of current *Syria* contains the following additional titles:

SCHAEFFER: Les fouilles de Ras Shamra (Ugarit). Sixieme campagne. Pp. 141–176.

DUSSAUD: Deux stèles de Ras Shamra portant une dédicace au dieu Dagon. Pp. 175–180.

Les éléments déchainés. Une application des règles rythmiques phéniciennes. Pp. 196–205.

A propos de la Table dite généalogique. Pp. 207–208.

VIROLLEAUD: Sur quatre fragments alphabétiques. Pp. 180–187.

GASTER: The Ras Shamra Text "TG". Pp. 225–227.

Journ. Pal. Or.. Soc. 1935:

GINSBERG and MEISLER: The Ewirizar Lẹtter. A Reply. Pp. 181–184.

TEXTS

NOTE: There are, of course, no special final forms of letters in the Ras Shamra alphabet. The Hebrew final forms ך, ם, ן, ף, ץ are used here only for convenience of reading. In the following ( ) signifies a break which has been filled in on the basis of parallel passages; ⟨ ⟩ signifies an omission of the scribe; | | signifies an error of the scribe which should be omitted; a point under a letter indicates that the letter is doubtful.

A

לבעל Sup. i

×ר | באב⟨ן⟩ | תד(י) (פ)סלתם (ביער)
תהדי | לחם | ודקן (תתלת)
קן | שרעה | תחרת | כם | גן
אפלב | כעמק | תתלת | במת
בעל | מת | מי | לאם | בן דגן
מי | המלת | אתר | בעל | נרד
בארץ | עמה | תרד | נרת
אלם | שפש | עד | תשבע | בך
תשת | כין | אדמעת | גם
תצח | לנרת | אלם | שפש
עמס מע | לי | אלאין | בעל
תשמע | נרת | אלם | שפש
תשא אלאין | לכתף
ענת | כתשתה | תשעלינה
בצררת | צפען* | תבכינה
ותקברנה | תשתנן | בחרת
אלם | ארץ | תטבח | שבעם
ראמם | כגמן | אלאין

l. 16: Scribal error for צפן?

(ב)על | תטבח̄ | שבעם | אלפם
(כג)מן | אלאין | בעל
(תט)בח̄ | שבעם | צאן
(כגמ)ן | אלאין | בעל
(תט)בְח̄ | שבעם | אילם
(כגמן) | אלאין | בעל
(תטבח̄ | ש)בעם | יעלם
(כגמן | אל)אין | בעל
(תטבח̄ | שבעם |) חִמרם

Col. i

. . . א | אלאין | בעל . . .
. . . . חה | פשתבם | ע . . .
. . . זרה | יִבם | לאלם
(אד)ך | לתתן | פנם | עם
(א)ל | מבך נהרם | קרב —
(א)פק | תהמתם | תגלי | ש̄ד
אל | ותבא | קרש
מלך | אב | שנם | לפען
אל | תהבר | ותקל
תשתחוי | ותכבדנה
תשא | גהִ | ותצח | תשמח̄הת
את̄רת | ובנה | אלת | וצב
רת | אריה | כמת | אלאין
בעל | כח̄לק | זבל | בעל
ארץ | גם | יצח | אל
לרבת | את̄רת ים | שמע
לרבת | א(ת̄רת) ים | תן
אחִד | ב | בנ . ך אמלכן
ותען | רבת | את̄רת ים

בל | נמלך | ידע | ילחן
ויען | לטפן | אל ד‹פ›א
ד | דק אנם | לירפע
עם | בעל | ליעדב | מרח
עם | בן | דגן | כתמסם
וען | רבת | אתרת ים
בלת | נמלך | עתתר | ערץ
ימלך | עתתר | ערץ
אפנך | עתתר | ערץ
יעל | בצררת | צפן
יתב | בכחת | אלאין
בעל | פענה | לתמ×ין
הדם | ראשה | לימ×י
אפסה | ויען | עתתר | ערץ
לאמלך | בצררת | צפן
ירד | עתתר | ערץ | ירד
לכחת | אלאין | בעל
וימלך | בארץ | אל | כלה
.... שאבן | ברחבת
..... שאבן | בככנת

Col. ii.

ל...
ול...
כד | ...
כד | ת...
יעתקן | כ...
תנגתה | כלב | א(רח)
לעגלה | כלב | תא(ת)
לאמרה כם | לב | ענ(ת)

אתר | בעל | תאחד | מ(ת)
בסאן | לפש | תשצק
בקץ | אלל | תשא | גה | ו(תצ)
ח | את | מת | תן | אחי
וען | בן | אלם | מת | מה
תארשן | לבתלת | ענת
אן | אתלך | ואצד | כל
צר | לכבד | ארץ | כל | גבע
לכבד | שדם נפש | חסרת
בן | נשם | נפש | המלת
ארץ | מ×ת | לנעמי | ארץ
דבר | יסמת | שד | שחלממת
נגש | אנך | אלאין בעל
עדבנן אנך | אמר | בפי
כללא | בתבר נקי | חתאהו
נרת | אלם שפש | צחררת
לאשמם | ביד | בן אלם | מת
ים | ימם | יעתקן | לימם
לירחם | רחם | ענת | תנגתה
כלב | ארח | לעגלה | כלב
תאת | לאמרה | כם | לב
ענת | אתר | בעל | תאחד
בן | אלם | מת | בחרב
תבקענן | בחתר | תדרי
נן | באשת | תשרפנן
ברחם | תטחנן | בשד
תדרענן שארה | לתאכל
עצרם | מנתה | לתכלי
נפר . אר | לשאר | יצח

col. iii

כחִלק | זְבִ(ל בעל ארץ)
והם | חי | א(לאין בעל)
והם | אתֿ | זבל | בע(ל ארץ)
בחלם | לטפן | אל | דפאד
בשׂרת | בני | בנות
שמם | שמן | תמטרן
נחלם | תלך | נבתם
ואדע | כחי | אלאין בעל
כאתֿ | זבל | בעל | ארץ
בחלם | לטפן אל דפא(ד)
בשׂרת | בני | בנות
שמם | שמן | תמטרן
נחלם | תלך | נבתם
שמח | לטפן | אל | דפאד
פענה | להדם | יתפד
ויפרק | לצב ויצחק
ישא | גה | ויצח
אתבן | אנך | ואנחן
ותנח | בארתי | נפש
כחי | אלאין בעל
כאתֿ | זבל בעל ארץ
גם | יצח | אל | לבתלת
ענת | שמע | לבתלת | ענ(ת)
רגם | לנרת | אל | שפ(ש)

col. iv

פל | ענת | שדם | י שפש
פל | ענת | שדם אל | ישתך
בעל | ענת | מחרתת
אי | אלאין | בעל

אי | זבל | בעל | ארץ
תתבע | בתלת | ענת
אדך | לתתן | פנם
עם | נרת | אלם | שפש
תשא | גה | ותצח
תחם | תר | אל | אבך
הות | לטפן | חתכ . .
פל | ענת | שדם | י שפש
פל | ענת | שדם | אל | י(שתך)
בעל | ענת | מחרתה
אי | אלאין | בעל
אי | זבל | בעל | ארץ
ותען | נרת | אלם | ש(פש)
שדין | ען | ב | קבת . .
ב . לית* | על | אמתך
ואבקת | אלאין | בעל
ותען | בתלת | ענת
אן | לאן | י שפש
אן | לאן | אל | יקר . .
ת×רך | ש
ישתד
אר
ר

l. 43: In ב . לית either ד or ל or א.

col. v

יאחד | בעל | בן | אתרת
רבם | ימחץ | בכתף
. כים* | ימחץ | בצמד

l. 3: דכים or אכים.

צחֿרמתֿ | ימצאֿ | לארץ
. . . רֿ . ץ | לכסאֿ | מלכה
. . . . לכחתֿ | דרכה
י . . . | לירחֿם | לירחֿם
לשנת | . . . בֿשבע
שנת | ורֿךֿ | בן | אֿלם | מת
עם | אלאֿין | בעל | ישאֿ
גה | ויצח | עלך | . . ם
פהת | קלת | עלך | פהת
דרי | בחרב | עלך
פהת | שרף | באֿשת
עלך | (פהת | ט)חן | ברח
.ם | עלך פ(הת) . . חֿ | בֿרֿברת
עלך | פהת . צחֿ . .
בשדם | עלך | פהת
.דרע | בים | ן | . .
באחֿר | . ספא* | ויתֿב
אך | דנֿר . . . אֿם
אחד | בא . . לֿ . . .
.נ . | אחצֿ . . .
. . ם | אכל | . . .
. כלי | המל . . .
ו . . עֿל | א . . .
ש . . .
בל . . .

l. 20: אֿספא or הספא.

. . . . ר̣דה col. vi
. . . . ר̣שה
. . . . ר̣א
. . . .
. . . . מ̣ת
. . . . מר | לאמם
. . . . . . בן | אלם | מת
. . א . שבעת | ×למה
. . ת̣ | בן | אלם | מת
. . ן | אחים | יתן | בעל
לפאי | בנם | אמי | כליי
יתב | עם | בעל | צררת
צפן | ישא* | גה | ויצח
אחים | יתנת | בעל
לפאי | בנם | אמי | כל
יי | יתען | כגמרם
מת עז | בעל | עז | ינגחן
כראמם | מת | עז | בעל
עז | ינתכן | כבתנם
מת | עז | בעל | עז | ימצחן
כלסמם | מת | קל
בעל | קל | עלן | שפש
תצח | למת | שמע | מע
לבן | אלם | מת | אך | תמתח
ץ | עם | אלאין | בעל
אך | אל | ישמעך | תר
אל | אבך | ל | יסע | אלת
תבתך | ליהפך | כסא | מלכך
ליתבר | חט | מתפטך

l. 13: ישל in text.

ירד | בן | אלמת | ח̄תע | י
דד | אל | ×זר | יִער מת
בקלה | י . . .
בעל | יתח̄בן . . .
מלכה | . לר . . .
דִרכתה . . .
. . . . נ . . .
. . . ען | הנ . . .
. . . . . . שנת . . .

sup. vi
. . . . פְאִת
. . . . תְקבאת
. . . . . ר | אנשת
. . . . תְא | לתשת קל
. . . | טרי | אף | לתלחם
(ל)חִם | תרממת | לתשת
ין | ת×צ̄ית | שפש
רפאם | תחתך
שפש | תחתך | אלנים
עדך | אלם | הן | מתם
עדך | כת̄רם | חברך
וח̄סס | דעתך
בים | ארש | ותנן
כת̄ר | וח̄סס | יד
יתר | כת̄ר | וח̄סס

ספר אלמלך שבני
למד | אתן | פרלן | רב
כהנם רב | נקדם
ת̄עי | נקמד מלך אגר(ת)
אדן ירגב | בעל | ת̄רמו

B

col. i

.

.

.

. . . . ⟨יצ⟩ח | ת֯ר

⟨א֯ל | אבה | א֯⟩למלך

. . . .

. . . . . . | את֯

⟨רת⟩. . . . מ֯לת

. . . . ה

. . . .

. . . .

. . . .

מתב א֯ל | מצ֯לל

בנה | מת֯ב | רבת

את֯רת | ים | מת֯ב

כלת | כנית

מת֯ב | פדרי | ב⟨ת⟩אר

מצ֯לל | טלי | בתרב

מת֯ב | ארצי | בת | יעבדר

אף֯ | מת֯ן | רגמם

ארגמך | שסכן מע

מגן | רבת | את֯רת ים

מ×ק֯ | קנית | א֯לם

הין | עלי | למפח֯ם

בד | ח֯סס | מצבטם

יצק | כסף֯ | ישל

ח | חרץ | יצק | כסף
לאלפם | חרץ | יצק
ם | לרבבת |
יצק | חים | ותבתח
כת | אל | דת | רבתם
כת | אל | נבת | בכסף
שמר זת | בדם | חרץ
כחת | אל | נחת
בצר | הדם | אל*
דפרשא | בבר
נעל | אל | ד | קבלבל
עלן | יבלהם | חרץ
תלחן | אל | דמלא
מנם | דבבם | ד
מסדת | ארץ
צע | אל | דקת | כאמר
סכנת | כחות | ימאן
דבה | ראמם | לרבבת

l. 35: אד in text.

col. ii

. ב . . .
. אבנ . . .
אחדת | פלכה . . .
פלך | תְעלת | בצמ . . .
נפינה | מכס | בשרה
תמתע | מדה | בים | תו
נְפינה | בנהרם
שתת | חפתר | לאשת
חברת | לצר | פחמם

תעפף | תר | אל | דפאד
ת×צי | בני | בנות
בנשא | ענה | ותפהן
הלך | בעל | אתתרת
כתען | הלך | בתלת
ענת | תדרק | יבמת
. . . . . | בְה | פענם
. . . . . . | דְן | כסל
. . . . נה | ת . . .
ת× . . . .
אנש | דִת | צר . . .
תשא | גה | ותצח | אך
מ×י | אלאין | (ב)על
אך | מ×ית | ב(ת)לת
ענת | מחצי אִמְחִץ
בני ה . . . . . צברת
אריי . . . כסף | בִרת
כתען | צל | כסף | ונ . . .
חרץ | שמח רבת | א(תרת)
ים | גם | ל×למה | . . .
ען | מכתר | אפ . . .
דגִי | רבת | אתר(ת ים)
קח | רתת | בדכת
רבת | על | ידם . . .
במדד | אל | . . .
בים | אל | ד . . .
הר | אל | י . . .
אלאין . . .
בתלת | . . .

מה | כְ . . .
ואת . . .
את̄ר . . .
באם . . .
בל | ל . . .
מלמְ . . .
דת . . .
בט . . .
גם . . .
י . . .

col. iii

.
. . . . דן
. . . . דד·
. . . . ן | כב
. . . . | אל | ינס
. . . . יסדך |
. . . . | דר | דר
. . . . יך | ורחד
. . . יאלם | דמלך
י . . | אלאין | בעל
י . . דד | רכב | ערפת
. . | ידד | ויקלצן
יקם | ויופת̄ן | בתך
·פ(ח̄)ר | בן | אלם | שתת
פְ . . בת̄לחני | קלת
בְכס | אשתינה
. ם | ת̄ן | דבחם | שנא | בעל | ת̄לת̄

רכב | ערפת | דבח
בת̄ת | ודבח | ודבח̣*
דנת | ודבח | תדמם
אמהת | כבה | בת̄ת | לתבט
ובה | תדממת | אמהת
אח̄ר | מ×י | אלאין | בעל
מ×ית | בתלת ענת
תמגנן | רבת | את̄רת ים
ת×צ̄ין | קנית אלם
ותען | רבת | את̄רת ים
אך | תמגנן | רבת
את̄רת | ים | ת×צ̄ין
קנית | אלם | מגנתם
ת̄ר | אל | דפאד | הם | ×צ̄תם
בני | בנות ותען
בתלת | ענת | נמגן
נ̣ם | רבת | את̄רת | ים
. ×̣צ̄ | קנית | אלם
. . . | נמגן | הות
. . | אלאין | בעל
. . | רבת | את̄רת | ים
. . | בתלת | ענת
. . (תל)ח̣ם | תשתי
. . . . . ע | מר×ת̄ם
. . . . חת | קץ
. . . . רפנמין
. . . . | עצם
. . . .

l. 19: Second ודבח by dittography.

. . . .
. . . .
. . . .
. . . .
. . . . על .
. . . . לן

col. iv ת̄ר
את̄ר(ת) . . .
ואת̣ . . . .
את̄רת׳ ים . . .
צמד | פחל | . . . .
כסף | דת | ירק . . .
עדב | גפן | אתנת̣(ה) . .
ישמע | קד⟨ש⟩ | ואמר
מדל | ער | צמד | פחל
שת | גפנם | דת | כסף
דת | ירק | נקבנם
עדב | גפן | אתנתה
יחבק | קדש | ואמרר
ישתן | את̄רת | לבמת | ער
ליסמסמת | במת | פחל
קדש | יאח̄דם | שבער
אמרר | ככבכב | לפנם
את̄ר | בתלת | ענת
ובעל תבע | מרים | צפו
א̄דך | לתתן | פנם
עם | א̄ל מבך | נהרם

קרב | אפק | תהמתם
תגלי | שׂד | אל | ותבא
קרש | מלך | אב | שנם
לפען | אל | תהבר | ותקל
תשתחוי | ותכבדנה
הלם | אל | כיפהנה
יפרק | לצב | ויצחק
פענה | להדם | ית̄פד | ויכרכר
אצבעתה | ישא | גה | וי(צח)
אך | מ×ית | רבת | את̄ר(ת | י)ם
אך | אתות | קנית | א(לם)
ר×ב | ר×בת | ו . . ת .
הם | ×מא | ×מאת | ועס . . .
לחם | הם | שתים | לח(ם)
בת̄לחנת | לחם | שת(י)
בכרפנם | ין | בך* | ח̄רץ .
דם | עצם | הם | יד | אל מלך
יח̄ססך | אהבת | ת̄ר | תעררך
ותען | רבת | את̄רת ים
תחמך | אל | חכם | חכמת
עם עלם | חית | חצ̄ת
תחמך | מלכן | אלאי(ן) | בעל
ת̄פטן | ואן | דעלנה
כלנין | ק . . . . .
כלנין | .בִל | כסה
. . . . יצח | ת̄ר אל | אבה
(א)לִמלך | דיכננה | יצח
את̄רת | ובנה | אלת | וצברת

l. 37: Probably בכ⟨ס⟩.

אריה | ון | אן | בת | לבעל
כם אלם | וחצר | כבן | אתרת
מתב אל מצלל | בנה
מתב רבת | אתרת | ים
מתב | כלת | כנית
מתב | פדרי | בת אר
מצלל | טלי בת רב
מתב | ארץ | בת יעבדר
ויען לטפן אל דפאד
פעבד | אן | ענן | אתרת
פעבד | אנך | אחד אלת
הם | אמת | אתרת | תלבן
לבנת יבן | בת | לבעל

col. v
כם אלם | וחצר | כבן | אתרת
ותען | רבת | אתרת ים
רבת | אלם | לחכמת
שבת | דקנך | לתסרך
רחנתת | ד . | לארתך
ונאף | עדן | מטרה
. על | יעדן | עדן | תכת | בגלת
ותן | קלה | בערפת
שרה | לארץ | ברקם
דת | ארזם | יכללנה
הם | בת | לבנת | יעמסנה
לירגם | לאלאין | בעל
צח | חרן | בבהתך*
עשבת | בקרב | הכלך

l. 75: בבהמך in text.

תבלך | ×רם | מאד | כסף
גבעם | מחמד | חרץ
יבלך | אדר | אל | קצם
ובן | בהת | כסף | וחרץ
בהת | טהרם | אקנאם
שמח | בתלת | ענת | תדעץ
פענם | ותר | ארץ
אדך | לתתן | פנם
עם | בעל | מרים | צפן
באלף | שד | רבת | כמן
צחק | בתלת | ענת תשא
גה | ותצח | תבשר בעל
בשרתך | יבלת | יבן
בת | לך | כם | אחך | וחצר
כם | אריך | צח | חרן
בבהתך | טשבת | בקרב
הכלך | תבלך | ×רם
מאד | כסף | גבעם | מחמד |
חרץ | ובן | בהת | כסף
וחרץ | בהת | טהרם
אקנאם | שמח | אלאין
בעל | צח | חרן | בבהתה
עשבת | בקרב הכלה
יבלנן ×רם | מאד | כסף
גבעם | מחמד* | חרץ
יבלנן | אדר אל קצם
יאכל כתר | וחסס

ותבלם ספר || כתלאכן

l. 101: לחמד in text.

×למם

אח̄ר | מ×י | כת̄ר | וח̄סס
שת | אלף | קדמה | מרא
ותך | פנה | תעדב | כסא
ויתת̄ב | לימן | אלאין
בעל | עד | לחם | שת(י) . .
ויען | א . . | . . . .
. . . ב . . . .
(ח)ש | בהתם | . . .
חש | רמם | ה . . .
חש | בהתם | תבן . .
חש | תרממן | ה . . .
בתך | צררת | צפן
אלף | שד אח̄ד בת
רבת | כמן | הכל
ויען | כת̄ר | וח̄סס
שמע | לאלאין בעל
בן | לרכב | ערפת
בל | אשת | ארבת | בבה(תם)
חלן | בקרב | הכלם
ויען | אלאין בעל
אל | תשת | ארבת | ב(בהתם)
(חל)ן | בקרב | הכ(לם)

col. vi

ויען | כ(ת̄ר | וח̄ס)ס
תת̄ב | בעל | ל . . .
ת̄ן | רגם | כ(ת̄ר | ו)ח̄סס
שמע | מע | לא(לא)ין בעל
בל | אשת | אר(בת) | בבהתם

חלן | בקרב (| הכ)לם
וען | אלא(ין |) בעל
אל | תשת | א(רב)ת | בבהתם
חלן | בק(רב | הכ)לם
אל | ת . . . . . . | בת אר
. . . . | בת | רב
. . . . דד | אלים*
. . . . . לצן | ופתם
. . . . ויען | כתר
(וחסס | ת)תב | בעל | להותי
. . . בהתה | תבנן
. . . תרמם | הכלה
י . . | ללבנן | ועצה
ל . . ין | מחמד | ארזה
ה . (ל)בנן | ועצה
ש . . ין | מחמד | ארזה
תשת אשת | בבהתם
נבלאת | בהכלם
הן ים | ותן | תאכל
אשת | בבהתם | נבלאת
בהכלם | תלת | רבע* ים
תאכל (| (א)שת | בבהתם
נבלא(ת |) בהכלם
חמש | ת(ד)ת | ים | תאכל
אשת | (ב)בהתם נבלאת
ב(הכלם) . . . לם | מך
בשב(ע |) ים . | תד | אשת

l. 12: Or אל[י]ם, with י a scribal error?

l. 26: כבע in text.

בבהתם | נ(בל)את | בהכלם
סב | כסף | לרקם | חרץ
נסב | ללבנת | שמח
אלאין | בעל | התיבנת*
דת | כסף | הכלי | דתם
חרץ | עדבת | בהת . . . ל
יעדב | הד | עדב . . . ת
הכלה | טבח | אלפם . . .
צאן | שקל | תרם . . .
ראא | אל | עגלם | ד . .
שנת | אמר | קמץ | . . אם
צח | אחה | בבהתה | א(ר)יה
בקרב הכלה | צח . .
שבעם | בן | אתרת . .
שפק אלם | כרם | י . .
שפק | אלהת | חפרת . .
שפק | אלם | אלפם | י . .
שפק | אלהת | ארחת . .
שפק | אלם | כחתם | י(ם)
שפק | אלהת | כסאת . .
שפק | אלם | רחבת ין
שפק | אלהת | דכרת* . .
עד | לחם | שתי | אלם
ופק | מר×תם | תד . .
בחרב | מלחת | קב . .
א | תשתי | כרפ(נם י)ן
. . . .

l. 36: Perhaps ⟨ב⟩התי בנת.

l. 54: Last letter may be ן.

. . . . ן
. . . . ת
. . . . ת̆
. . . .
. . . .

col. vii

. . . . קנא . .
. . . . . . אלאין | בעל
. . . . . .תך | מדד אל
י . . . . .לצ̆ר | קדקדה
אל . . . . . חק ·| ב×ר
כם | י . . . אלם | בצפן
עדר | ל . . ערם
ת̆ב | לפד(ר |) פדרם
ת̆ת̆ | לת̆ת̆ם | אח̆ד | ער
שבעם | שבע | פדר
ת̆מנים | בעל | מ . . . .
תשעם | בעל | מר . .
ב . . . . | בעל | בקרב
בת | ויען | אלאין
בעל | אשתם | כת̆ר בן
ים | . . ר | בנם | עדת
יפתח | חלן | בבהתם
אר(ב)ת | בקרב הכל
ם | ו(פ)תח | בדקת | ערפת
על פ . . | כת̆ר | וח̆סס
צחק | כת̆ר | וח̆סס
ישא | גה | ויצח
לרגמת | לך | לאלא

ין | בעל . ת . בן | בעל
להות | יפתח | ח
לן | בבהתם | ארבת
בקרב | הכ(לם | יפ)תח
בעל | בדקת (| ערפ)ת
קלה | קדש | . . . . תן
ית̄ני | בעל | צ̣ . . . פ̣תה
קלה | ק . . . . ר | ארץ
. . . . ת̣×רם | אח̄שן
רתק . . . .
קדמים | במת | א . . .
תטטן | א̄ב | בעל אא̄ח̄ד
יערם | שנא̄ | הד | פת
×ר | ויען | אלא̄ין
בעל | א̄ב | הדת̣ | לם | תח̄ש
לם | תח̄ש | נת̄ק | דמרן
ען | בעל | קדם | ידה
כת×ש̄ | ארז | בימנה
בכם | ית̄ב | בעל | לבהתה
א̄מלך | א̄בלמלך
ארץ | דרכת ישתכן
ד̣לל | אל | א̄לאך | לבן
א̄לם | מת | עדד לידד
א̄ל | ×זר | יקרא | מת
בנפשה | יסתרן ידד
בגנגנה | אחדי | דימ
לך | על | א̄לם | לימרא
א̄לם | ונשם | דישב

. המלת | ארץ | גם | ל×
(למ)ה | בעל | כיצח | ען
(גפן) | ואגר | ב×למת
(עממ)ים | בן | צ̄´למת | ר
. . . . . . א̄בר . נת
. . . . ע̣רפת
. . . . חת
. . . . ם
. . . .
. . . . ף

fragment parallel to end of
B col. vii

. כ מגן | רבת | אח̄רת
| מ×ק̄ | קנית | א̄לם
. . תתן בת | לבעל | כם
(א̄)לם | וחצ̄ר | כבן
(א)ח̄רת | גם | ל×למה
ב̣על | יצח | ען | גפן |
ואגר | בן | ×למת
עממים | בן | צ̄למ(ת)
רמת | פרעת | א̄בר
צחררם | חבל . .
ערפת | תחת | . .
מעצרם | ח . .
גלח̄ | א̄סר . .
ם | ברת . .
ימת . .
שא̄ . .
מ . .

col. viii

א̄דך | אל | תתן | פנם
עם | ×ר | תר×זז
עם | ×ר | ת̄רמג
עם | תלם | ×צר | ארץ
שא | ×ר | על | ידם
ח̄לב | לצ̇ר | רחתם
ורד | בתח̄פת̄ת
ארץ | תספר | בי
רִדם | ארץ
א̄דך | אל | תת̇ן
פנם | תך | קרתִה
המרי | מך | כסא̄
ת̄בתה | ח̄ח̄ | ארץ
נחלתה | ונ×ר
עתִן | א̄לם | אל
תקרב | לבן | א̄לִם
מת | אל | יעדבכם
כא̄מר | בפה
כללא̄ | בת̄בר נִ
קנה | תח̄תאן
נרת | א̄לם | שפש
צחררת | לא
שמם | ביד | מד
ד | א̄לם | מת | בא
לפ̄ | שד | רבת | כ
מן | לפען | מת
הבר | וקל
תשתחוי | וכ
בד הות | ורגם

לבן | אלם | מת
ת̆ני | לידד
אל | אזר | תחם
אלאין | בעל
. . . . . . ת | אלאי | ק
. . . . בהתי בנת
. . . . ח̆י
. . . . אח̆י
. . . . אח̆י
. . . . י
. . . . ב
. . . . חת
. . . . ת
. . . . | אלם
. . . . אי̇ד
. . . . . . ד
. . . . . . ד̣ אגר

. . . . ת
. . . .

alongside of col.

. . . (ת̆)עי | נקמד | מלך אגרת

C

אקרא | אלם | נ(עמם)
ויסמם | בן | שר(ם)
יתנם | קרת | לעל . . . .
במדבר | שפם | יד . . . . ר
לראשהם | ויש . . . . . . ם
לחם | בלחם. י ושתי | בחמר ינאי
שלם תמלך | שלם | מלכת | ערבם | ותננם

מת | ושר | יתב | בדה | חט | תכל | בדה
חט | אלמן | יזברנן | זברם גפן
יצמדנן | צמדם | גפן | ישקל | שדמתה
כם גפן

שבעד | ירחם | על | עד | וערבם | תענין

ושד | שד אלם | שד אתרת | ורחם
על | אשת | שבעד | ×זרם | טב(ח ג)ד | בחלב | אננח | בחמאת
ועל | אגן | שבעדם | ד× . . . . . ת

תלכם | רחמי | ותצד. . .
תחגרן | ×זר נעם . . .
. תשם | ערבם | יר . . .

מתבת | אלם | תמן | ת . . .
פאמת | שבע

אקנא | שמת
(ב)ן | שרם |

אקראן | אלם | נעמם . . . . ים
ינקם | באף זד | את̄רת | . . .
שפש | מיפרְת | דלתהם . . .
ו×נבם | שלם | ערבם | ת̄נ(נם)
הלכם | בדבח | נעמת

שד אלם | שד | את̄רת | ורחמי
. . . | י . ב

. . . . ב . | גף ים | ויצמְד | גף | תהם
. . . . . לְף משתְעלתם | משתְעלתם | לראש | אגן
הלה . שהל הלה | תרם | הלה | תצח | אד אד
והלה | תצח | אם | תארכם | יד | אל | כים
ויד | אל | כמדב | ארך | יד | אל | כים
ו | יד | אל | כמדב | יקח | אל | משתְעלְתם
משתְעלתם | לראש | אגן | יקח | יש⟨תְ⟩ | בבתה
אל | ח̄טה | נחת אל | ימנן | מט | ידה | ישא
יר | שממה | יר | בשמם | עצר | יח̄רט ישת
לפחם | אל | את̄תם | כיפת | הם | את̄תם | תצחן
ימת | מת | נחתם | ח̄טך | ממננם | מט ידך
ה(ל) עצר | תחהר | לאשת | צחררת | לפחמם
א(ת̄)תם | את̄ת | אל | את̄ת | ועלְמה | והם
א(ת̄)תם | תצחן | י | אד אד | נחתם | ח̄טך
ממננם | מט ידך | הל | עצר | תחרר | לאשת
וצחררת | לפחמם | בתם | בת | אל | בת | אל
ו(ע)למה | והן | את̄תם | תצחן | י | מת | מת
נחתם | ח̄טך | ממננם | מט ידך | הל | עצר
תחרר | לאשת | וצחר(ר)ת | לפחמם | את̄תְם | א(ת̄ת אל)
א(ת̄)ת | אל | ועלמה | יהבר | שפתהם | יש . . .
הן | שפתהם | מתקתם | מתקתם | כלרמן . .
. ם | נשק | והר | בחבק | חמחמת | תקת(נצן)

תלדן | שחר | ושלם | רגם | לאל | יבל | א(תתי)
אל | י(ל)ת | מה | ילת | ילדי | שחר | ושל(ם)
שא | עדב | לשפש | רבת | ולכבכבם | כנ . . .
יהבר | שפתהם | ישא | הן | שפתהם | מתקת(ם)
בם | נשק | והר (| ב)חבק | וח(מ)חמת | יתבנ . . .
יספר | לחמש | ל . . . . . שר | פחר | כלאת
תקתנצן | ותלדן | תלד (ן אלם |) נעמם | אגזרים
בן | ים | ינקם | באפ . ד . רגם | לאל | יבל
אתתי | אל | ילת | מה | ילת | אלם י נעמם [אגזר]*
אגזרים | בנים | ינקם | באף | שד | שת | שפת
לארץ | שפת | לשמם | ו . ערב | בפהם | עצר | שמם
ודג בים | ונדד | . . . ל . . | יעדב | אימן
אשמאל | בפהם | ולדשבעני | אתת | אתרח
יבן | אש . ד* | שא | עדבתך | מדבר קדש
תם | תגרגר | לאבנם | ולעצם | שבע | שנת
תמת | תמן | נקפת | עד | אלם | נעמם | תתלכן
שד | תצדן | פאת | מדבר | ונגש | הם | נ×ר
מדרע | ו . חהם | עם | נ×ר | מדרע | י | נ×ר
נ×ר | פת . | ופתחהו | פרץ | בעדהם
וערב | ה . . | המ . . . . ם | ותן
ונלחם | הם | את . . . . . . תן | ונשת
וענהם | נ×ר מדרע . . . . . ת
את | ין | דערב | בתכ . . . .
מ×אפת | להן | לג ינה . . . .
וח . רה | מלא ין . . .

l. 60: Last word erased by scribe.

l. 65: In אש . ד either ל or ד or א.

D

col. i

כתמח̄ץ | לתן | בת̄ן | ברח
תכלי | בת̄ן | עקלתן
שליט | ד | שבעת | ראשם
תת̄כח | תתרף | שמם | כרס
אפדך | אנך אספא | אטם
שׂרקם | אמתם | לירת
בנפש | בן אלם | מת | במה
מרת | ידד | אל | ×זר
תבע | ול | ית̄ב אלם | אדך
ליתן | פנם | עם | בעל
מרים | צפן | ויען
גפן | ואגר | תחם | בן אלם
מת | הות | ידד | בן* אל
×זר | פנה | ש | נפש | לבאת
תהו | הם | ברלת | אנח̄ר
בים | הם | ברכי | תכשד
ראמם | ען | כשד | אילת
הם אמת אמת | נפש | בלת
חמר | . התת | בכלאת
ידי | אלחם | הם | שׁבע
ידתי | בצע | הם | כס | ימסך
נה . כל | צחא בעל עם
אח̄י . ואן | ה.* | עם | אריי

l. 13: [בן] may be a scribal error, to be omitted.

l. 23: הד or הב.

ולחמ .* עם | אח̄י | לחם
ושתת . עם | א . ין*
פנօשת | בעל | ענ֯אטענך
. . . . תօאօ . . . ך | כתמח̄ץ
. . . . ח | תכלי
. . . . שליט
. . . . ת̄תכח
. . . . ך

l. 24: ולחמםօ, perhaps ולחמתօ.

l. 25: Perhaps א(ח̄)ין, for אח̄י ין.

. . . . ם col. ii
. . . . . רץ | שפת | לשמם
. . . . שן | לכבכבם | יערב
. . ל | בכבדה | בפה ירב
כחרר | זת | יבל | ארץ | ופר
עצם | יראאן | אל֯אין | בעל
ת̄ק | נן* | רכב ערפת
תבע | רגם | לבן | א֯לם | מת
ת̄ני | לידד א֯ל ×זר
תחם | אל֯אין | בעל | הות | אל֯אי
קרדם | בהת̄ | לבן | א֯לם מת
עבדך | אן | ודעלמך
תבע | ול | ית̄ב | א֯לם א֯דך
ליתן | פן | עם | בן | א֯לם | מת
תך קרתה | המרי | מך | כסא֯
ת̄בתי | ארץ | נחלתה | תשא
גהם | ותצח | תחם | אל֯אין

l. 7: Perhaps ת̄תעׄו|[נן.

בן* | בעל | הות | אלאי | קרדם

בהת̄ | בן | אלם | מת | עבדך | אן

ודעלמך | שמח̄ | בן אלם | מת

. . . ה | ואצח | אך | ילחן

. . . . י . ר* | אנהד

. . . . ף | מלחמי

. . . . לת | קצ̄ב

. . . . שמחי

. . . . בע

. . . . נג .

l. 18 [בן] may be a scribal error, to be omitted.

l. 22: יתִר, perhaps יאִר.

col. iii

. . בת | ת̄בת | ת . . .

רבת | ת̄בת | ח .* . . .

י | ארץ | חשנ . . .

תעתד | תכל . . .

תכן | לבנ . . .

דת | לבנך . . .

דך | כ | כבכבִ . . .

דם | מת | אצחִ . . .

ידד | בקר(ב) . . .

אל | אשת | בִ . . .

אהפך | ל . . .

ת̄מם | ולך . . .

ולך | אלם . . .

נעם | אלם . . .

שגר | מא . . .

l. 2: חשִ or חעִ.

שגר | מא . . .
דם | מת | אצ(ח) . . .
יד* | בקרב . . .
ולך | אלם . . .
ורגם | ל . . .
במאד | צא . . .
מאד | צאן . . . .
אתם | מאא . . .
דם | מת | אצ(ח) . . .
ידד | בקר(ב) . . .
תמם | ולך | . . .
. . ת | לך . . .
. . כת | א . . .

l. 19: יד⟨ד⟩?

col. iv

פשנ . . .
ולטלב . . .
מאת | רח . . .
תטלב | א . . . .
ישא | גה . . .
א | אף | בע* . . .
א | הד | ד . . .
ינפע | בע . . .
בתמנת | . . .
יקרב | . . .
לחם | מ . . .
. דלחם . . .
ופקמ . . . .

l. 6: בע(ל)?

בּחרב . . .
ש . יכר* . . .
. כסח̄ר* . . .
כס | כס .* . . .
כרפן | . . .
ותת̄תנ .* . . .
תעל | תר .* . . .
בת | אל | לא . . .
על | חבש | . . . .
מן | לאך | . . .
לאך | תל . . .
תעדרן . . .
נ . .* | פ . . . .

l. 15: After ש, either ת, or א or נ.

l. 16: Perhaps (ב)כס.

l. 17: Perhaps ם at break.

l. 19: י or ח̄ at break.

l. 20: ש or ע at break.

l. 26: Second letter ה or א; third letter צ or ב.

col. v

. . . . אלאין
. . . . .ף | דפרך
. . . . מ̇נך | ששרת
. . . . ת | נפש | עגל
. . . . נ̇ך | אשת | ן | בח̄רת
אלם | ארץ | ואת | קח
ערפתך | רחך | מדלך
מטרתך | עמך | שבעת
×למך | ת̄מן | ח̄נזרך

עמך | פדרי | בת | אר
עמך | תטלי | בת | רב | אדך
פנך | אל תתן | תך ×ר
כנכני | שא | ×ר. על ידם
חלב | לצר | רחתם ורד
בתחפתת | ארץ | תספר בי
רדם | ארץ | ותדע אלל
כמתת | ישמע | אלאי* | בעל
יאהב | עגלת | בדבר | פרת
בשד | שחלממת | שכב
עמנה | שבע | לשבעם
ת . . לי* | תמן | לתמנים
ו . . . רן | ותלדן מת
אל . . . . *שלבשן
א . . . . לה | מ×צ
י . . . . | לארתה

l. 17: Probably ⟨אלאי⟨ן⟩⟩ with ן omitted by error.

l. 21: Second letter ש or ע.

l. 23: Before שׁ either ל or ד.

col. vi

. . . . א
. . . . שנם
. . . . ח | סבן
. . . . . . ת . . עדך
כסם | מהית | (מ)×ני
לנעמי | ארץ | דבר
ליסמת | שד | שחלממת
מ×ני | לבעל | נפל | לא

רץ | מת | אלאין | בעל
חלק | זבל | בעל | ארץ
אפנך | לטפן | אל
דפאד | ירד | לכסא | יתב
להדם . ץ | הדם | יתב
לארץ | יצק | עמר
אן | לראִשה | עפר | פלתת
ל | קדקדה | לפש | יכס
מאזרתם | ×ר | באבן
ידי | פסלתם | ביער
יהדי | לחם | ודקִן
יתלת | קן | שרעה | יחרת
כגן | אפלב | כעמִק | יתלת
במת | ישא | גה | ויצח
בעל | מת | מי | לאם | בן
דגן | מי | המלת | אתר
בעל | ארד | בארץ | אף
ענת | תתלך | ותצד | כל | ×ר
לכבד | ארץ | כל | גבע
לִ(כ)בִד | שדם | תמ× | לנעם
. . . דבר | יסמת | שד .*
(שחל) ממת | ת . . לבעל | נ פּ .*
. . . . *. . . . . . | תכס | מא . .

l. 29: Probably nothing after שד.

l. 30: It is not certain that there is a letter missing after נפּ

l. 31: Third or fourth letter of line is either כ or ר.

GLOSSARY

Citations:

A = Virolleaud, *Syria* xii, 1931, plus 'Fragment nouveau,' *Syria* xv, 226 ff.

B = Virolleaud, *Syria* xiii, 1932

C = Virolleaud, *Syria* xiv, 1933

D = Virolleaud, *Syria* xv, 1934

T = Virolleaud, *Syria* x, 1929, 304 ff.

T^2 = Dhorme, *Syria* xiv 229 ff. (two tablets)

T^3 = Virolleaud, *Syria* xv, 75 ff. ('Traité hippologique')

T^4 = Virolleaud, *Syria* xv, 148 ff.

T^5 = Virolleaud, *Syria* xv, 244 ff. (3 tablets)

"H." indicates Biblical Hebrew roots. Pointed Hebrew words are those of the Biblical lexicon. The order of arrangement is in general by roots. Cross reference is made to Biblical citations in cases of interest in text and correspondence in interpretation.

א

א = אוֹ *either, or* (?): אימן אשמאל, C 63–64. See also under ו.

אב = אָב *father*: אבך A vi 27, אבה B iv 47; אב שנם title of 'El A i 8 (cf. אבי עד, Is. 9:5).

אב = אוֹיֵב *enemy*: אב בעל || שנא הד, B vii 35; אב הדת, l. 38.

אבמן n. pr. T^5 1 margin.

אבן = אֶבֶן *stone:* pl. אבנם ועצם, C 66 (cf. I Ki. 5:32); . . . ביער באבן, A sup. i 2 = D vi 17.

אבר = אֵבֶר *feather*: רמת פרעת אבר, B vii 56 and fragm. 9; see פרע.

אגזרי C 58, 61.

אגן = אַגָּן *basin*: C 15, 31, 36.

אגר *Ugar*, patron deity of Ugarit: גפן ואגר, B vii 54 and fragm. 7, viii 47, D i 12; see גפן.

אגרת *Ugarit*: T 2:18 f; בת א' T 2:27; T[2] 1:11; נקמד מלכאגרת B viii colophon.

אגרתי n. gent. T[5] 1: 8, 9.

אד a divine title, *father*: reduplicated אדאד || אם אם C 32–33, || מתמת C 43–46.

אדך *then* (Arab. *'idāk*, cf. אָז): אדך לתתן פנם A iv 31, B iv 20, v 84; אדך אל תתן פנם B viii 1; אדך ליתן פנם D i 9–10, ii 13, v 12.

אדן = אָדוֹן *lord*: A sup. vi 57.

אדר = אֶדֶר *glory*: B v 79.

אהב *to love* (H): יאהב D v 18.

אהבת = אַהֲבָה *love*, B iv 39.

אהף: יאהף || יראש, T[3] A rev. 1, both of equine maladies.

אורנר n. pr. (Hurrian): T 15:5.

אורשר n. pr.: T[2] 2:11, = Hurrian *Iwri-šarri* in the Ḳatna inventory, Syria XI, 313 (cf. אורנה 2 Sam. 24:16, אֲרַוְנָה הַמֶּלֶךְ v. 23).

אזמר material for divine thrones: T 3:51, = Akk. ešmarū (?) (= חשמל?); see ששר.

אזר: מאזרתם D vi 17.

אחד = אֶחָד *one*: A i 18.

אחדי *I alone*: B vii 49.

אחרה *together*: T[3] A, B (cf. יַחְדָּו).

אח = אָח *brother*: אחי *my brother* A ii 12, as ritual cry B viii 37 ff.; אחך B v 90; אחה B vi 44; pl. אחים A vi 10, 14; pl.+suff. אחי || אריי D i 23.

אחד = אָחַז *to take hold of:* pf. אחדת B ii 3; impf. יאחד A v 1, תאחד A ii 9, 30, pl. יאחדם B iv 16; אחד B vii 8, vii 9.

. . . אחצ̆ A v 23.

אחר = אַחַר *afterwards, after:* B iii 23.

אטם see טם(?).

אי = אֵי *where:* A iv 28.

איל = אַיִל *ram*, or אַיָּל *stag*: A sup. i 24.

אילת = אַיֶּלֶת *doe?*; pl. אילת D i 17.

אך A v 21.

אך = אֵיכָה *how, where, why:* A vi 24 ff., B ii 21, 23, iii 28, iv 32, D ii 21.

אכל = אָכַל *to eat:* תאכל B vi 24; Pi. יאכל B v 103.

אל = אַל *not:* always with juss. A vi 26, B iii 5; אל יעדבכם *lest he make you* B viii 7; אל תשת *do not set* B vi 8.

אל = אֵל *god*, in sing. always of the supreme god El, as A i 7, or of the deity of a named place, as אל דפאד; Mot is ידד אל B vii 46, מדד אל B vii 4; pl. אלם B i 23, vi 47, C 1, 13, 60; בן אלם = בְּנֵי אֵלִים, בְּנֵי אֱלֹהִים B iii 14; Mot is בן אלם A ii 13, מדד אלם B viii 23; in אלים B vi 12 is י scribal error?; אלהם in Tabb., as T 1:3 (as distinct deity?—cf. Heb., and Sanch. Ελωειμ); fem. אלת *goddess*, generally title of אתרת, A i 12; cf. also T 1:11; pl. אלהת B vi 48. Elision of א in ענתלתן T 9:17?

אלן *god* (Phoen. אלן): אלנים (י scribal error?) A sup. vi 46.

אל = אֶל *to?*: אלקצם B v 79.

אלאין *Aleyan*, deity; always+בעל: א' בעל A i 1; = בעל A v 1, A i 23 || בן דגן A i 24; also זבל בעל ארץ, רכב ערפת. Construct case אלאי: אלאי קרדם B viii 34, D ii 10–11, 18.

אלל *lamentation?* (cf. אַלְלַי Mic. 7:1): A ii 11.

אלל *lamentation?*: D v 16.

אלם : אלמן = אַלְמָן *barreness*; see תכל.

אלמלך = אֱלִימֶלֶךְ n. pr.: A sup. vi 54.

אלף = אֶלֶף *ox*: B v 107; pl. B vi 40.

אלף = אֶלֶף *thousand*: pl. || רבבת B i 28; *people* T[2] passim (cf. Is. 60:22).

אלקצם see אל II.

אלשי = אֱלִישָׁה *'Alašiya-Cyprus*: T2:9, 12:21.

אלשתמעי n. gent.: (cf. n. loci אֶשְׁתְּמוֹעַ also אֶשְׁתָּאֹל; for -אל cf. אֵל בֵּית אֵל and S. Arab. אלמקה *god of oracle*) T[5]1: 29 ff.

אלה : אלת תבתך A vi 27.

אם = אִם *if*, or interrogative particle?: T[2] 2:14.

אם = אֵם *mother*: אמי A vi 11, אם אם C 33.

אמר : כאמר B i 42.

אמר *lamb* (Akk. immeru): A ii 8.

אמר(ר?) *Amurru*, genius of the Amorites: קדש ואמרר B iv 8, 13, 17.

אמת = אָמָה *maid*: א' אתרת B iv 61; pl. אמהת B iii 21.

אמת : הם אמת אמת D i 18.

אמת *word*? (Akk. amātu, awātu): על אמתך A iv 43.

אן = אָן *whither*: A ii 15 (or = אָנָּא *ah!*); אן לאן A iv 46 47 (cf. אָנָה וָאָנָה, 1 Ki 2:36).

אן see אנך.

אן || צמא : D i 23.

אן = אַיִן, אֵין *is not*: B iv 44, 50, T[2] 2: 9.

אן D vi 15, see עמר.

אנחר *snorter*, a sea animal (= W. Sem. in Akk. naḫīru): אנחר בים D i 15.

אנך = אָנֹכִי *I*: A ii 21, B iv 60, D i 5; אן = אֲנִי(?) A ii 22, D ii 12, 19.

אנם = אוֹנִים *strength?*: A i 22.

אנח || נגד?: C 14.

אנף: אף = אַף *nostril*: pl. יצק באפה T[3] A obv.; באף *at, in front of*, in prepositional phrase C 24, 61, see חד (cf. Eth. 'af).

אנש: אנשת A sup. vi 40.

אנת: אחת = אֵשֶׁת *woman, wife*: dual אחתם C 39, 42, 43, 46, 48; cst. אחת אל C 42, 48.

אף = אַף *moreover:* B i 20; ונאף B iv 68, see נ.

אפלב in parallelism with במת A sup. i 5 = D vi 21.

אפנך *then* (Akk. appūna): A: 28, D vi 11.

אפס *extremity*: אפסה *his feet* A i 33, v 20 (cf. אָפְסַיִם).

אפק = אָפִיק *stream*: A i 6 (cf. Job 38:16).

אקנא *lapis lazuli* (Akk. uḳnu)?: אקנאם B v 81, 97. But see also קנא.

אר = אוֹר *light* (?) in בת אר a temple name: B i 17, iv 55, D v 10; see פדרי.

ארב: ארבת = אֲרֻבָּה *lattice-window:* B v 123, vii 18.

ארז = אֶרֶז *cedar*: pl. B vi 19; בת ארזם B v 72 (cf. 2 Sam. 7:2).

ארח *wild-cow*: A ii 6, 28; pl. ארחת B vi 50 (cf. Akk. arḫu).

ארי in pl. *associates*: +suff. אריה A i 13 || בנה; אריך B v 91 || אחך, B vi 44, B ii 26; אריי || אחי D i 23; (cf. n. pr. אֲרִיאֵל Ezra 8:16, so also with Gr. in 2 Sam. 23:20; cf. אֶרְאֶלָּם || מַלְאֲכֵי שָׁלוֹם, Is. 33:7; שְׁנֵי אֲרִאֵל מוֹאָב, 2 Sam. 23:20?).

ארך = אָרַךְ *to stretch, extend*: C 34, תארכם C 35; ארכתה *its extent* A vi 35 (or read דרכתה).

ארץ = אֶרֶץ *earth*: C 62 || שמם; ארץ אל A i 57; זבל בעל ארץ A i 15; postpositive to place-names B viii 4; בחרת אלם ארץ (*burial place?* cf. O. Aram. ארצתא) A sup. i 18.

ארצי a deity: B i 19 = B iv 59 (where ארץ; cf. Hadad inscr. l. 11: ארקרשף and Palmyrene רצו as divine names; cf. Earth as deity in Sanch.); or *my land*, see פדר.

ארש *to desire*: תארשן A ii 14 (cf. אֲרֶשֶׁת Ps. 21:3).

ארש *desire?*: בים ארש ותנן A sup. vi 50.

ארת *breast* (Akk. irtu): A iii 19, B v 67.

אשו[ד]ד *Ashdod?* (or אשלד): C 65.

אשחת a deity T 17:9.

אשחר *Išḫara*, Bab. deity: T 1:13, Syria XII. 389, l. 7.

אשכני n. gent. (cf. אַשְׁכְּנַז?): T^5 1:22 ff, T^5 2 rev. 3.

אשס = אֲשִׁישׁ a raisin cake, etc., as remedy: T^3 B 14.

אשת = אֵשׁ *fire*, אִשֶּׁה *fire-sacrifice*: A ii 33, B ii 8, vi 22, 25, C 14, 41.

אשמני *Eshmun, Eshmunite* (?): בעל בת א' T 14:2.

את = אַתָּה *thou*: A ii 12, D v 6.

אתו = אָתָה *to come*: אתות B iv 32.

אתן = אָתוֹן *she-ass*: pl. אתנתה B iv 7, 12.

אתן פרלן n. pr.? A sup. vi 54.

אתרח n. pr.? C 64; = תרח *Teraḥ?* in Syria xiv, 149, n. 1 (unpublished text).

את = יֵשׁ (Aram. אִיתַי, Akk. išū) *there is*: A iii 3, 9, 26, C 74.

אתר *place, sanctuary* (Akk. ašru): א' אתרת T 8+31:7; א' אלם T 5:24; B iv 18; ענת א' בעל *Anat the Place* (i. e. surrogate) *of Baal* A ii 9, 30 (see זבל; cf. Heb. מָקוֹם); אתר בעל A sup. i 7 = D vi 24–25.

אתרת = אֲשֵׁרָה *Athirat-Ashera*: A i 12, C 13 generally רבת א' ים A i 16; = אלת A i 12, קנית אלם B i 23, mother of the gods B vi 46; A v 1, B iv 61, C 24, 60, T 9:8 (cf. Jud. 3:7, 1 Ki. 18:19, 2 Ki. 21:7, 23:24; in Teima inscr. אשירא).

אתתרת: בעל א' (error?) B ii 13 (cf. Jud. 10: 6).

ב

בּ = ב *in*: A i 29, ובה B iii 22; *among* בכם B vii 42; *of* בלחם, בחמר C 6 (or = מִ־); A i 18, see בן = מִן.

בד = בַּד *portion*: T 18:19–21; בדם חרץ? B i 33 (cf. Ex. 30:34).

בד = בִּידֵי? B i 25 (and T 18:19–21?); see יד.

בדלית (or בללית) A iv 43.

בדק = בֶּדֶק *aperture*: בדקת || ארבת || חלן B vii 19, 28.

בהת see בת.

בהת D ii 11, 19.

בוא *to enter* (H): תבא A i 7.

בות = בּוֹשׁ *to be ashamed*: דבח בתת (= בֹּשֶׁת) *sacrifice of shame* B iii 19,21.

בין *to understand, pay heed* (H): impr. בן || שמע B v 122.

בכי = בָּכָה *to weep*: תבכינה *she bewept him:* A sup. i 16.

בך = בְּכִי *weeping*: A sup. i 9.

בל = אֲבָל, (Phoen. בל, Arab. bal) *nay rather*; also בלת: בל || בלת A i 20, 26.

בלת see בל.

בלת D i 18.

במת *top, back?*: B iv 15 (cf. בָּמָה?); *high places?* in contrast to עמק A sup. i 5 = D vi 21; לבמת *on the back of* (cf. עַל־בָּמֳתֵי) B iv 14.

בן = מִן *from?*: A ii 18; ב = מִ־ *of, among?* אחד ב בנך A i 18 (cf. confusion of these prepositions in Phoen., S. Arab. and in Heb. text of Bible with Gr. interpretation).

בן = בֵּן *son*: מנם ובנה T 15:11; *citizen?* C 65; of parentage of gods A i 24, A ii 13; pl. בן אלם B iii 14, B vi 46; dual? בנים C 59, 61; f. dual בתם C 45.

בני = בָּנָה *to build*: pf. בנת B viii 35; juss. pass. יבן B iv 62; תבנן B vi 16; impv. בן B v 122; here too בני בנות || אל דפאד A iii 5, B ii 11, iii 32?

בעד = בַּעַד *for*, prep.?: בעדהם C 70; Shafel? שבעד C 12, 14, 15.

בעי (?) *to seek*: תבע B iv 19, D i 9, ii 8, 13; Hitp. תתבע A iv 30 (or probably better תבע *to follow*).

בעל = בַּעַל *proprietor*: בת . . .ובעלה T 15:1–2, A sup. vi 57; of gods as possessors of particular places, sanctuaries, attributes בעל צפן A i 14, זבל ב' ארץ A i 4, cf. T 1:10, T 14; בעל כנף T 9:6; pl. בעלם following אלהם T 1:9; particularly title of Aleyan אלאין בעל A i 1; as distinct name *Baal* לבעל title A sup. i 1; בעל מת A sup. i 6 = D vi 23; בן || אתר בעל דגן A i 24, A sup. i 7 = D vi 25; ב' ואתרת T 9:8; fem. בעלת בהתם T 1:21, cf. T 3:37, T 33:7.

בער = בָּעַר *to burn*? (Arab. bǵr): Shafel שבער B iv 16.

בצע D i 21 (*to divide*? cf. Heb.).

בקל *grain* (cf. S. Arab., Akk. buḳlu): קמח בקל T³ A rev. 3.

בקע = בָּקַע *to cleave*: תבקענן A ii 32.

בקעתי n. gent. from בִּקְעָה: T⁵ 3:5.

בקת = בִּקֵּשׁ *to seek*: אבקת A iv 44.

בר *fine cloth*?: דפרשת בבר B i 36.

ברח = בָּרַח *fleeing* : D i 1, see לתן.

ברך: ברכי D i 16.

ברלת: D i 15.

ברק = בָּרָק *lightning*?: B v 71.

בשר = בָּשָׂר *flesh*?: B ii 5.

בשר = בִּשַּׂר *to bring good news*: תבשר and noun בשרתך = בְּשֹׂרָה B v 88–89.

בת = בַּת *bath*, a liquid measure: בת . . . שמן T 3:20.

בת=בַּיִת *house*: בת ארזם B v 72; T 5:2; in temple names בתרב (Akk. ēkallu) B i 18, iv 56, vi 11; בתאר, see אר; בת יעבדר B i 19, iv 57; pl. בהת B v 75 ff,. vi 38; בהתי B viii 35; בהתם B v 113, 115, T 1:21? · For form בהת cf. S. Arab. in Rhodokanakis, *Studien* I, p. 12 ff.

בתחפתת see חפת (?).

בתלת=בְּתוּלָה *virgin*: title of ענת A ii 14.

בתן *serpent* (cf. פֶּתֶן): A vi 19; D i 1, 2, see לתן.

ג

גבע=גֶּבַע *heap, hill*: A ii 17, B v 78.

גג=גַּג *roof*: T 3:50 (cf. 2 Ki. 23:12—or *top* of altar, cf. Ex. 30:3).

גד=גְּדִי *kid?*: see טבח.

גד=גַּד *Luck*(?): בגד צפן T² 1:10.

גדל=גָּדוֹל *great*: T 12:1; fem. גדלת of some large animal T 1.

מגדל=מִגְדָּל *tower* or place-name T 1:11.

גה *voice* (by context): A i 11; תשא גהם (particle גה+ם) D ii 17.

גור=גָּר *to sojourn*: Pilp. תגרגר C 66 (cf. הִתְגּוֹרֵר).

גזר see אגזרי.

גלי=גָּלָה *to wander over?*: תגלי A i 6, B iv 23.

גלת: בגלת B v 69, fragm. l., 13.

גם=גַּם *moreover*: A i 15, B ii 29, A sup. i 10.

גמן *to cover over* (Akk. kamânu)?: כגמן אלאין A i sup. 21 ff.

גמר: כגמרם || כראמם A vi 16.

גן=גַּן *garden*: תחרת כם גן A sup. i 4=D vi 21.

גנגן *chamber* (Akk. gangannu): B vii 49.

גער=גָּעַר *to roar*: יגער of a horse T³ B 23.

גף *inside? upon?*, prep.: גף ים || גף תהם C 30 (rt. גוף?).

גפן *harness?*: גפן אתנתה B iv 7, 10, 12.

גפן = גֶּפֶן *vine* C 9, 10, 11.

גפן *Gupn*, patron-deity of Gupn-Byblos; see אגר.

גפת *dome?*: גפת א×ר B vii 36.

גרגס n. pr. (cf. גִּרְגָּשִׁי?, Gen. 15:21) T[5] 1:29.

גרן- = גָּרוֹן, *throat?*: מכשר ג' T[3] A obv. 10.

ד

ד, fem. דת, relat.-demons. particle = זו, זֶה (e. g. Gen. 31:32), Arab. ḏû, Aram. ד, די: אל דפאד (?); דת כסף דת חרץ *the one of silver, the other of gold* B iv 10; B i 31, ii 20, D i 3; דתם (= דת+ם) B vi 37; עבדך אן ודעלמך (rt. עלם) D ii 12 = 19; rel. pron. דמלך *who reigned* B iii 9, דמלא *which is full* B i 39, דבה *in which?* B i 44, דעלנה *who is over him* B iv 44; ד תשמע *which you shall hear* T[2] 2:17; rel. conj. of purpose דיכננה B iv 48, דיקח T 3:20.

דבב B i 40.

דבח = זֶבַח *sacrifice*: B i 44, iii 18 ff.; דבח נעמת C 27 (cf. רֵיחַ נִיחֹחַ Eze. 6:13); pl. דבחם B iii 17; דבחן *our sacrifices* T 2:24, 32; verb impf. נדבחה T 2:24, 33.

מדבח = מִזְבֵּחַ *altar*: T 3:41; pl. מדבחת T 3:24.

דבלת = דְּבֵלָה *dried figs*: דבלת ישנת T[3] A rev. 2, B 33 || צמקם (also T 12:17?), used as a medical plaster, cf. דְּבֶלֶת תְּאֵנִים 2 Ki. 20:7.

דבר = דֹּבֶר *wilderness*: || שד שחלממת A ii 20, D v 18–19.

מדבר = מִדְבָּר *desert*: C 4, 68; במדבר קדש C 65.

דג = דָּג *fish*: דגבים C 63.

דגן = דָּגוֹן *Dagon*: T 9:3, 17:6; = *Aleyan* בן דגן || בעל A i 24, A sup. i 6 = D vi 23–24.

דד = דוד *pot*: T 3:44, 12:1.

דדמי name of a people: T 2:29, 17:5.

דוב = זוב *to flow*: מדב *flood* C 34, 35 || ים.

דוך *to bruise* (H): T³ A obv. 9, B 35 (cf. Nu. 11:8).

דך demonstrative, reported in Syria xiv p. 137, n. 2 (unpublished text).

דכי *to crush* (H. דָּכָה, cf. דָּכָא. דָּכַךְ): דכים A v 3 (or אכים)?

דכר = זָכָר *male*: T 5:19.

דכרן = זִכָּרוֹן *phallus*: pl. B vi 54 (cf. Is. 57:8).

דלל *guide*? (Arab. dalîl): B vii 45.

דלת: דלתהם C 25 (cf. דָּלִיּוֹת *boughs*?).

דם = דָּם *blood*: דם עצם B iv 38, a liquor; דם ין T 3:23 (cf. Gen. 49:11, Dt. 32:14); T 9:1; in B i 33?

דם: דם מת D iii 9, 18.

דמם *to wail* (H; Akk. damāmu): ודבח תדמם אמהת *and the sacrifice in which the maids wail* (for the dead vegetation god)? B iii 20, 22 (cf, Eze. 8:14).

דמע *to weep* (H): דמעת verb, or *tears* A sup. i 10.

דמר *to be awesome*? (cf. Aram.): דמרן B vii 39.

דנת *baseness* (cf. Arab. daniya) or *whore* (Heb. rt. זנה): B iii 20.

דעץ *to tread*? (cf. Arab. da'aṣa): תדעץ פענם B v 82.

דפאד in לטפן אל דפאד, a deity: A i 21 etc.

דפרן name of a tree?: T³ B 24 (cf. Akk. daprānu).

דק = דַּק *small*: דק אנם A i 22; דקת of some small animal T 1; דקת כאמר B i 42.

דקן = זָקָן *beard*: B v 66, A sup. i 3 = D vi 19.

דר = דּר *generation*: דר דר B iii 7 (cf. Ex. 3:15 etc.); *dwelling* דר בן אל (cf. Is. 38:12) T 2:17, T² 1:2; in temple name יעבדר B i 19?

דרי = זָרָה *to winnow*: תדרינן A ii 32; דרי A v 13.

דרך, דרכת *rule* (cf. uses of דֶּרֶךְ): דרכה (or דרכ[ת]ה) || מלכה A v 6; דרכתה (or ארכתה) A vi 35; דרכת *my rule* B vii 44.

דרע = זָרַע *to sow* (Arab. zara a but cf. Aram. variant דרע, S. Arab. דׄרא): A ii 35, v 19.

דרע = זֶרַע *seed* in a remedy: T[3] B 25.

מדרע *sown land*, see נ×ר.

דרק B ii 18.

ה

הבר: תהבר A i 9; impv. הבר B viii 27; יהבר שפתהם C 49, 55 (Hif. of ברר with retention of ה?; cf. הָבֵרוּ, לְהָבַר and GK § 53 q; in sense *to act piously* as in Arab., so S. Arab. stem IV?).

הד *Haddu* (cf. הֲדַד; S. Arab. הד): || בעל B vii 36, 38 (where הדת), D i 23, iv 7 (cf. הֲדֹרָם 2 Ch. 10:18, אֲדֹרָם).

הדי *to present, give* (=Arab.)?: יהדי D vi 19; תהדי A sup. i 3.

הדם = הֲדֹם *footstool* of gods (cf. Heb. ark): A i 32, iii 15, B i 35, iv 29, D vi 12.

הות *speech*(?): || תחם A iv 35, D i 13, ii 10; with suff. B vi 15, vii 24.

הות 3rd pers. pron.? (=Akk. šu'atu, S. Arab. הות Eth. we'etu; cf. Phoen. המת): כבדהות B viii 28 (cf. תכבדנה A i 10); תשמחׄהת? A i 11; נמגן הות B iii 36.

הין epithet of חׄסס *Ḫasis*: B i 24 (cf. Syriac הון *facile, handy*).

הכל = הֵיכָל *temple*: הכלך B v 76, הכלי vi 37 || התי <ב>; pl. הכלם B vi 23.

הל asseverative (or interject.) particle *behold*: C 41, 44, 48 (cf. B. Aram. אלו, O. Aram. הלו?).

הלה C 32, 33 (or *then*?).

הלך *to go* (H): pf. B ii 13, 14 (*perished?*, Arab. halaka); impf. תלך A iii 7; impv. לך B vii 23; ptcpl. הלכם C 27; Iftaal אתלך A ii 15, fem. תתלך D vi 26, pl. תתלכן C 67.

הלם = הֲלֹם *then* B iv 27.

הם *behold* (see הן): A iii 2, 3, B iii 31, iv, 61, v 73, C 39, T 13:5, 8, T² 2:9; D i 15, 16.

המל *to crowd?*: המלת A ii 18, B vii 52 (cf. הֲמֻלָּה); cf. A v 25; המלת || לאם A sup. i 7 = D vi 24.

המר see מהמרת.

המרי B viii 12 = D ii 15.

הן = הֵן *behold*: C 46 (variant to הם), 50, 55; הן ים *lo, one day* B vi 24.

הפך = הָפַךְ *to overturn*: ליהפך כסא A vi 28; +suff. אהפכך D iii 12.

הר = הַר *mountain*: B ii 36 (or נהר?).

הר *pruriency* (cf. הָרָה, הֵרוֹן Gen. 3:16, esp. הַרְהֹרִין Dan. 4:2; the place of this word in its context makes a meaning signifying a mental condition more suitable than *conception*, for which see קנץ): C 51, 56.

ו

ו = וְ— *and*, written separately C 35; perhaps א in אכים (if not דכים) A v 3 (see כי)?, cf. in T 2, e. g. תקטטן אתחטאן; אדמעת A sup. i 10.

ולד see ילד.

ופת: יקם ויופתן B iii 13.

ורך (?) A v 9.

ותר see ראי.

ז

זבל *Zebul* (*abode*, personified as deity): זבל בעל ארץ A i14 || אלאין בעל (cf. Heb. זְבֻל and n. pr. in [א]זבל; cf. also Phoen. nn. pr. in זבל).

זבר = זָמַר (Arab. zabara) *to trim*: יזברנן זברם גפן C 9.

זת = זַיִת *olive*: D ii 5.

זת: שמרזת B i 33.

ח

חבל fragm. l. 10.

חבק *to embrace* (H): B iv 13 (?); verbal noun C 51, 56.

חבר = חָבֵר *associate*: כתֿרם חברך וחֿסס דעתך A sup. vi 48.

חבר *vase* C 76 (Akk. ḫubūru).

חגר *to gird about* (H): ותחגרן . . . תצד (see יצד) C 16–17.

חדת = חֹדֶשׁ *new moon*: ים ח' תֿן *the second day of the new moon* T 3:48.

חות: כחות B i 43.

חי = חָיָה *to live*: חי *is alive* A iii 28; חית B iv 42?

חכם *to be wise* (H): חכם חכמת = חָכַם חָכְמָתָ? B iv 41; לחכמת B v 65.

חלב = חָלָב *milk*: C 14; see טבח.

חלל: חלן = חַלּוֹן *window*: B v 124, vi 6.

חלם = חֲלוֹם *dream*: A iii 4.

חמד: מחמד = מַחְמָד *desirable thing*: B vi 19, B v 78, 101 (cf. Hos. 9:6).

חמם *to be hot, concupiscent* (H): noun of reduplicated stem חמחמת C 51, 56 (cf. Is. 57:5, הנחמים באלים *who inflame themselves with the Els* rather than *among the terebinths*).

חמר = חֹמֶר *homer*, a measure: T 12:6, 12.

חמר = חֲמוֹר *ass:* חמרם A sup. i 28.

חמר D i 19.

חצ̇ר = חָצֵר *court?* (Arab. ḥaẓīrat): B v 63.

חצ̇ת B iv 42.

חרב = חֶרֶב *sword, knife:* A ii 31; B vi 57?, D iv 14.

חרר *to burn* (H): Pual C 41, 44, 47; *to wither* D ii 5.

חרת̄ = חָרַשׁ *to plough:* A sup. i 4 = D vi 20; מחרת̄ת *ploughland?* A iv 27, 38 (where מחרת̄ה).

חש a repeated exclamation B v 113–116 (cf. חוש *hasten?*).

חשב = חָשַׁב *to think:* T 13:7.

ח̄

ח̄ברת̄ a sacrificial object: B ii 9.

ח̄בת goddess *Ḫepa:* T 4:56.

ח̄בתי n. gent. T[5] 1:39.

ח̄ח̄ *Ḫaḫu* in Cilicia?: B viii 13.

ח̄ט *staff, sceptre* (Akk. ḫattu): A vi 29, C 8, 37, 47.

ח̄טא = חָטָא *to sin:* אתח̄טאן T 2:14, 15.

ח̄ים a metal?: יצק ח̄ים B i 30.

ח̄לב || אר× B viii 6, D v 14.

ח̄לק *to die* (cf. Eth.): A i 14.

ח̄מא: ח̄מאת = חֶמְאָה *curds:* C 14.

ח̄מר = חֶמֶר *wine:* C 6.

ח̄מש = חָמֵשׁ *five:* B vi 29, C 57; ח̄מש עשרה = חֲמֵשׁ עֶשְׂרֵה *fifteen* T 1:9; ח̄משם = חֲמִשִּׁים *fifty* T 12:6, 12.

ח̄נזר = חֲזִיר *pig* (Arab. ḫinzīr): ת̄מן ח̄נזרך D v 9.

ח̄סס *to think, inspire* (Akk. ḫasāsu)?: B iv 39; ח̄סס a divine genius = Akk. Ḫasīs (Intelligence) B i 25, paired with כת̄ר (which see), כת̄רם חברך וח̄סס דעתך A sup. vi 48–49; see also הין.

חסר = חָסֵר *to fail*: A ii 7.

חפר *kid* of animal (Akk. ḫurāpu): pl. חפרת B vi 48.

חפתר a sacrificial object? || חברת B ii 8.

חפת: רד בתחפתת (= רֵד בֵּית־)? B viii 7, D v 15.

חר: חרת *grotto, pit* (Heb. חר): בחרת אלם ארץ A sup. i 17, D v 5–6.

חר *Horus*?: עשתרת חר T 5:1, 5 (cf. עשתר כמש, Mesha, l. 17).

חרט *to pluck* (=Arab.): עצר יחרט C 38.

חרי = חוֹרִי *linen*?: חרי ילבש מלך T 5:23.

חרי = חֹרִי *Horites-Hurrians*: T 2:21.

חרן B v 75, 91, 98.

חרץ = חָרַץ *cut*: חרצן *axe*; see כהן.

חרץ = חָרוּץ *gold*: B i 27, T 5:10, 13.

חש = חוּש *to suffer* (or Aram. חוש *to perceive*?): אחש B vii 32; לם תחש B vii 38, 39.

חתא: B viii 20, A ii 23; חתא נחתא T[2] 2:7, נחתא l. 10.

חתי = חִתִּי *Hittite* (Akk. Ḫatti): T 2:21.

חתר *sieve*?: A ii 32.

ט

טב = טוֹב *good*: כסף טב T 5:12 (cf. Gen. 2:12).

טבח = טָבַח *to slaughter*: B vi 10, A sup. i 18 ff.; *to cook* (as in Arab.) טבח [גד] בחלב *cook* [*a kid*?] *in milk* C 14 (cf. Ex. 23:19; 34:26, etc.).

טהר = טָהוֹר *pure*: pl. abstr. טהרם B v 81, 96.

טחן = טָחַן *to grind*: A ii 34, v 15.

טלב *to seek* (cf. Arab.)?: תטלב D iv 4, ולטלב D iv 2.

טלי a deity: B i 18, iv 46; תטלי בת רב (error?) D v 11.

טם(?): אטם D i 5.

טען *to pierce* (H)?: אטענך D i 26.

טׄרי A sup. vi 42.

י *O* with vocative: written separately C 40, 69; together with following word A iv 25, 46, C 65; cf. B iii 9, C 60, 64.

יבל *to bring* (H): pf. יבלת B v 89; יבלהם B i 38; impf. pass.? תבלך B v 74, 93, יבלך v 79, יבלנן v 100, 102; רגם לאל יבל *word to El is brought*(?) C 52, 59. יבל=יְבוּל *produce*: יבל ארץ ופר עצם D ii 5.

יבם A i 3, B ii 15.

יד=יָד *hand*: יד אל C 33; יד אלם T² 2:11–12; ביד A ii 25, B viii 23; בד=בְּיַד? B i 25; בדה *in his hand*? C 8; ידה C 37; ימנה || ידה, B vii 40; pl. על ידם B ii 33, viii 5; ידן T 15:11; בכלאת ידי D i 19–20. Also ידתי D i 21?

יד A sup. vi 51.

ידד *to love*: יד *love* B iv 38 || אהבת.

ידד *beloved* title of Mot: ידד אל ×זר B vii 46, viii 31; cf. B iii 12 (cf. Sanch. Ιεδουδ, H. יְדִיד).

מדד *friend* title of Mot מדד אל B vii 4, מ' אלם B viii 23 (for form cf. מֹדָע).

ידע=יָדַע *to know*: ידעת T 13:21; אדע A iii 8, ותדע D v 16; ppl. ידע A i 20.

דעת *acquaintance*: || חבר, *associate*, A sup. vi 49; cf. S. Arab. מודת *friend* (of the king).

ילד=יָלַד *to bear*: ילת<ילדת C 53 (cf. Gen. 16:11); תלדן C 52, 58, D v 22.

ילד=יֶלֶד *child*: ילדי du. C 53.

ולד = וָלָד *offspring*: ולׂדׂ שבעני C 64.

ים = יוֹם *day*: B vi 47–58, A sup. vi 50; pl. ימם; as conj. *while* A ii 4, 26 (cf. Ps. 54:4); as a deity T 9:6; 17:8 (as in Sujin Aram. inscr. A a 12).

ים = יָם *sea*: A v 19, C 30; דג בים C 63, cf. D i 16; ים אל B ii 35 (cf. Eze. 28:2, 14, 16); אתרת ים *Athirat of the Sea* A i 16; cf. B vii 15.

ימן = יָמִין *right hand*: B v 109, vii 41; || שמאל C 63.

ין = יַיִן *wine*: B iii 43, iv 37, C 74, A sup. i 10; . . . לתלחם לחם לתשת ין A sup. vi 42–44; דם ין T 3:23 (cf. דם עצם).

ינק = יָנַק *to suck*: C 24, 59, 61.

ינת = יוֹנָה *dove*: T1:1.

יסד = יָסַד *to found*: מסדת = מוֹסָדוֹת *foundation* מ' ארץ B i 41 (cf. 2 Sam. 22:16); cf. B iii 6.

יסם *pleasant, gracious* (Arab. wasama, Akk. asāmu): || נעם A ii 20 = D v 7; נׂעׂמׂם ויסמם C 2.

יסר *to discipline, instruct* (H): לתסרך B v 66.

יעבדר name of temple B i 19.

יעל = יָעֵל *wild-goat*: יעלם A sup. i 26.

יער = יַעַר *forest*: pl. יערם B vii 7, 36; *wood* D vi 18.

יפר: שפש מיפרת C 25. (cf. Arab. wafara).

יצד? (cf. Arab. waṣada): C 16 (or root צוד), see חגר.

יצק = יָצַק *to fuse*: impf. יצק B i 26, 27 (cf. Ex. 25:12), יצקם B i 28; *to pour* D vi 14, T[3] A obv. 3; Shafel תשצק לפש A ii 10?

יר: יר שממה (rt. ראי *to see* or ירי *to shoot?*) C 38.

ירגב place name: A sup. vi 57.

ירד = יָרַד *to go, go down* (cf. Arab. warada, Jud. 11:3): impf. ירד A i 35, תרד A sup. i 8, ארד D vi 25, נרד A sup. i 7; impr. רד B viii 7 = D v 14; ppl. B viii 8–9; pf. וירדת T 1:20.

ירח̄ = יָרֵחַ *month*: a definite month ירח̄ תשרת T 9:11, [—] בירח̄ (with days 13, 14 itemized) T 3:1; pl. ירח̄ם A v 7, C 12.

ירח̄=יָרֵחַ *Moon* deity T 1:14; שפש וירח̄ T 5:11, 14.

ירק *gold* (cf. S. Arab.; ירקרק חרוץ Ps. 68:14): || כסף̇ B iv 6.

ירת: לירת D i 6.

ירת̄ = יָרַשׁ *to take possession*: noun רת̄ת B ii 32.

ישן = יָשָׁן *old*: דבלת ישנת, צמקם ישנם T^3 A rev. 2.

ישתד A iv 49.

ישתכן see כון.

יתן = נָתַן (Phoen. יתן) *to give*: pf. יתנת A vi 15 [4]; יתן A vi 10; juss. ליתן D i 10, ii 13; לתתן A i 4; תתן B viii 1; impr. תן A i 17, ii 12, C 72 (cf. Am. 4:1); cf. C 3.

מתנת = מַתָּנָה ritual *gift* T 1:2. (cf. Ex. 28:38).

יתר A sup. vi 52.

ית̄ב = יָשַׁב *to sit*: impf. ית̄ב A i 30; ת̄בע ול ית̄ב א̇לם D i 9, ii 13 (cf. יֹשֵׁב הַכְּרוּבִים); impr. ת̄ב B vii 8; Hif. תת̄בן B vii 24; cf. A vi 33.

ת̄בת = שֶׁבֶת *sitting*: אלת ת̄בתך A vi 28, כסא ת̄בתה B viii 13, ת̄בתי (error for ה_?) D ii 16; ת̄בת̄ D iii 23.

מת̄ב = מוֹשָׁב *seat* of deity (cf. Eze. 28:2, also cultic object in S. Arabia): B i 13, iv 52; pl. מת̄בת א̇לם C 19, ארבע מ' T 3:51.

כ

כ = כְּ_ *like*: A ii 7, vi 16-21; כם גן || כעמק A sup. i 4–5.

כם = כְּמוֹ *like*: B iv 51, C 11; כם גן A sup. i 4=כגן D vi 21.

כ = כִּי *for, that, when*: A i 13, iii 8, B iii 21, D v 17; cf. B v 104?, T^3 A rev. 1, B 12; *in order that?* כתשתה A sup. i 15; emphatic particle? כיצח B vii 53, כיפת C 39 (cf. Gen. 18:20).

כבד = כָּבֵּד *to honor*: Pi. תכבדנה A i 10, תכבדה B iv 26, וכבדהות B viii 28; מתנת מנכבד T 3?;

כבד with preposition *within*: לכבד (Akk. ina kibitti) A ii 16, 17, בכבדה D ii 4.

כבכב = כּוֹכָב (Akk. kabkabu): B iv 17, D iii 8; pl. כבכבם C 54, D ii 3.

כד = כַּד *pitcher*: כדם ין T 3:23.

כהן = כֹּהֵן *priest*: לרב כהנם (address of a letter) T 18:1; same on five hatchets, see Syria x pl. lx; רב כהנם A sup. vi 54–55; כהנם || קדשם small tablet at end of A sup. vi.

כון *to be set* (H): תכן D iii 6; Polel דיכננה B iv 48; ישתכן loan-word from Akk. šutakunu B vii 44?

כנת *truth*? (Akk. kittu): בכנת אל T[2] 1:17?

כחת *seat*: A i 30, 36; || הדם B i 34; כחתם || כסאת B vi 51; לכחת דרכה || כסא מלכה A v 6.

כי: אכים? but see דכי.

כיפת C 39, see פתי.

ככנת || רחבת A i 38.

כל = כֹּל *all*: A ii 15; בארץ אל כלה A i 37; כלהם T 5:26.

כלאת *both* (cf. כִּלְאַיִם, Akk. f. kelāti): C 57; בכלאת ידי D i 19–20.

כלבי n. pr. T[2] 2:5 (cf. Bib. nn. pr. from rt. כלב).

כלי = כָּלָה *to be finished*: Pi. *to destroy* תכלי D i 2; לתכלי A ii 36, v 25 (cf. כַּלֵּה Ps. 59:14).

כליי A vi 11, 15.

כלל = כָּלַל *to wall about* or *to complete* (cf. S. Arab.): בת ארזם יכללנה B v 72.

כלנין B iv 45, 46.

כלת = כַּלָּה *Bride*, fem. deity (Akk. kallatu): B i 16, iv 54.

כם *so*: A ii 8 (cf. כֵּן).

כם *like*, see כ *like*.

כמן = כַּמֹּן *cummin?*: T 12:9.

כמן name of temple?: רבת כ' B v 86, 119, viii 25.

כמרב *Kumarba*, Hurrian father-god, in Hurrian Tab. T 4.

כנית: כלת כנית B i 16, iv 54; parallelism requires a temple name.

כנכני: ×ר כנכני D v 12–13.

כנף = כָּנָף *wing*: בעל כנף *Winged Baal* T 9:6 (cf. Prov. 1:17 and the winged Ashur-symbol).

כס = כּוֹס *cup*: B iii 16, and read בכרפנם || בכ<ס> חרץ B iv 37; כס ימסך D i 21; D iv 16, 17.

כסא = כִּסֵּא *throne*: כסא תבתה B viii 12, D ii 15, [כ]סא אלת T 23:2, תעדב כסא B v 108; כסא מלכך A vi 28; לכסא מלכה A v 5; pl. כסאת B vi 52; see כסֿא (a variant spelling).

כסי = כָּסָה *to cover*: יכס D vi 16.

מכס = מִכְסֶה *covering*: B ii 5?

כסף = כֶּסֶף *silver*: B i 26; שקל כ' טב T 5:12, 15.

כסֿא: כסֿא בעלת T 33:7, see כסא.

כרם: D i 4.

כרפן *cup* (Akk. karpu): || כס pl: כרפנם ין B iii 43, vi 58, D iv 18.

כרר *to encircle, twirl* (H): Pilpel יכרכר (cf. מְכַרְכֵּר 2 Sam. 6:14) B iv 29.

כשד *to conquer* (Akk. kašādu)?: D i 16.

כשר: מכשר T^3 A obv. 10 (cf. Arab. kasara, *to break*).

כשֿד D i 17.

כת: כת אל B i 31, 32.

כתמסם A i 24.

כתף = כָּתֵף *shoulder*: A v 2; לכתף . . . תשא A sup. i 14.

כת×ש B vii 41.

כתר *Kothar* a genius aligned with חסס: B v 103, 106, 120; vi 1, 3, 14; vii 20, 21, A sup. vi 51, constituting a binome, thus אשת sing. B v 123; in Sanchuniathon Χουσωρ, the first to build ships, etc.; כתר בן ים B vii 15; כתרם A sup. vi 48; cf. Phoen. names עבדכשר, מתנכישר and Heb. כָּשֵׁר *apt*; for form cf. כּוֹשָׁרוֹת Ps. 68:7 (and fem. Χουσαρθις in Sanch.).

מכתר B ii 30?

ל

ל particle of asseveration, with pf. (Akk. lû): לרגמת B vii 23; with impf. לאמלך A i 34; לתלחם . . . לתשת A sup. vi 42–43.

ל = לְ_ *to, for*: A i 3, C 41, לבעל title A sup. i 1; *at, on* . . . תשא לכתף A sup. i 14; יתב בעל לבהתה B vii 42; תגרגר לאבנם C 66 (cf. 1 Sam. 22:7, 23:10); with pronouns לי A sup. i 12, לך T² 2:4, לכם T 13:13, להם C 75.

ל conj. of purpose, with juss. (Arab. li): לתתן A i 4; לשלם לך T² 2:4 (cf. Hadad inscr. ll. 23, 24, 30, 31).

ל of vocative address?: A ii 14, iii 23, B v 121, 122.

לא = לֹא *not*: A ii 25, B viii 22.

לאך *to send*: אלאך B vii 45; לאך D iv 23, 24; impv. לאך T² 2:10; B v 104 (cf. מַלְאָךְ).

לאם *people* (=sing. of לְאֻמִּים): || המלת A sup. i 6 = D vi 23; לאמם A vi 6.

לאת = לֶאָה *ewe*?: C 57 but see כלאת.

לב = לֵב *heart*: A ii 7; כלבה T 3:52 (cf. נְדִיב לֵב Ex. 35:21).

לבאת = לְבִיָּא *lioness*(?): D i 14.

לבן: לבנת = לְבֵנָה *brick*: B iv 62, v 73, vi 35 (where perhaps לְבֹנָה *incense*); denom. vb. תלבן B iv 61.

לבנן = לְבָנוֹן *Lebanon*: B vi 18, 20.

לבש = לָבֵשׁ *to clothe self*: T 5:22.

לג = לֹג *log*, a fluid measure: לג ינה *the measure of his wine* C 75.

לחם *cheeks* (Heb. לְחִי)?: לחם ודקן A sup. i 3 = D vi 19.

לחם = לֶחֶם *food*: B iv 35, D i 24; denom. vb. = לָחַם *to eat* C 6, 72; לתלחם . . . לתשת A sup. vi 42–43; אלחם D i 20, cf. D i 24. מלחם: מֹלחמי D ii 23.

לחן: ילחן A i 20, D ii 21.

לטפן a deity (cf. Arab. laṭif *kindly*): ל' אל דפאד A i 21, iii 4; see דפאד, פאד.

לל = לַיִל *Night*, deity: T 1:12 (cf. Sujin inscr. A a 12).

ללא *kid* (Akk. lalu'u): A ii 23, B viii 19.

למד *to learn* (H): למד Piel = לִמֵּד *taught* (him) or לִמֻּד *pupil* (*of*) A sup. vi 54.

לסם *to gallop* (Akk. lasāmu): ppl. pl. A vi 20.

לפש A ii 10, D vi 16.

לצב *grief*?: A iii 16.

לקח *to take* (H): impf. יקח C 35, 36; impv. קח B ii 32, D v 6.

לרמן *grape* (Akk. luremētu)?: מתקתם כלרמן C 50.

לתח a grain measure (= לֶתֶךְ?): T 12.

לתן identical with לִוְיָתָן Leviathan: כתמחץ לתן בתן ברח תכלי בתן עקלתן D i 1–2; cf. Is. 27:1.

מ

מ enclitic particle (= Akk. –ma, S. Arab. –m): to verb יצק כסף לאלפם חרץ יצקם לרבבת B i 28; to noun תשא גהם D ii 17; to pronoun <ב>התי בנת דת כסף הכלי דתם חרץ B vi

36–38. What is taken as the plural ם_ (or 3rd pers. pl. suff.) in these texts may frequently be this particle.

מאד = מְאֹד *much*: מאד צאן D iii 22, 23; מאד B v 77, 94.

מאן B i 43.

מאת = מֵאָה *hundred*: T 22:10; pl. מאת T 12:3, 5.

מגן *to protect*? (cf. מָגֵן) || צי×: Pf. מגנתם B iii 30; impf. תמגנן iii 25, 28, נמגננהם iii 33, נמגן הות iii 36; noun? מגן i 22.

מד: מדה B ii 6.

מדב see דוב.

מדל: מדל ער || צמד פחל B iv 9; מדלך מטרתך D v 7, see רח.

מה = מָה *what*: מה תארשן A ii 13; מה ילת C 53.

לם = לָמָּה B vii 38, 39.

מהית (?) D vi 5.

מהמרת D i 7–8.

מות *to die* (H): Pf. מת A i 13 = D vi 9, B vii 34, A sup. i 6 = D vi 23; מתת 2nd pers? (מַתָּה Ez. 28:8) D v 17; Hif.+suff. אמתם D i 6?; ppl. מתם? A sup. vi 46; כמתם? T² 2:12.

מחץ = מָחַץ *to smite* (S. Arab. מחץ) A v 2, 3, = D i 1, read ימחצן in A vi 20?; Hift. תמתחץ A vi 24, מחצי אמתחץ B ii 24.

מט see נטה.

מטר *to rain* (H): A iii 6.

מטרת *rain* (cf. מָטָר): pl. D v 7, see רח.

מי interrogative particle (cf. מִי יָקוּם יַעֲקֹב Am. 7:2, 5; Ruth 3:16): A sup. i 6, 7 = D vi 23, 24.

מך B vi 31, viii 12 = D ii 15.

מלא = מָלֵא *full*: מלא ין *full of wine* C 76.

מלח: בחרב מלחת B vi 57.

מלך = מָלַךְ *to reign*: A i 27, 34, B iii 9; Hif. נמלך A i 26, אמלכן A i 18; inf. מלכך A vi 28, מלכה A v 5.

מלך = מֶלֶךְ *king*: מלכאגרת B viii colophon, A sup. vi 56; in royal ritual T 5:23; divine A i 8, מלכן *our King* B iv 43.

מלכם = מִלְכֹּם (also מַלְכָּם) *Milcom*, in list of deities T 17:11.

שלם מלכת ערבם C 7?

מם = מַיִם *water*?: אן מם T^2 2:9.

מן *vessel* (Phoen. מן, B. Aram. מאן)?: תלחן אל דמלא מנם B i 39.

מן: מן לאך D iv 23.

מנם *whatever* (Akk. minummē)?: T^2 2:15.

מנם n. pr.: T 15.

מנן *to act graciously with*? (Arab. manna IV) || נחת: Pa. ימנן מט ידה C 37, 40; ptcpl. used verbally ממנגם מט ידך (cf. Est. 5:2) C 40, 44.

מנת = מְנָת *portion, fate* (cf. מְנִי Is. 65:11): || שארה A ii 36.

מסך *to mix* (H): כס ימסך D i 21 (cf. כס . . . מסך Ps. 75:9).

מע iterative particle?: שמע - מע. A vi 23, B vi 4; שסכנמע B i 21; עמסמע A sup. i 12.

מען = מַעַן *sake*?: מענך T^2 2:15.

מצא *to attain* (H. מָצָא): Hif. ימצא לארץ A v 4.

מצח: ימצחן A vi 20 and in an unpublished text, Syria xiii 162 n. 2; see מחץ.

מר = מֹר *myrrh*: שמן מר T 12:8.

מרא = מְרִיא *fatling* || אלף B v 107; verb לימרא B vii 50 ?

מרח A i 23 (see רפע), T^2 1:12.

מת *Mot*, deity, enemy of Aleyan Baal: A ii 12, B vii 47; usual title בן אלם מת A ii 13; also מדד אלם מת B viii 23–24 (cf. A ii 25), ידד אל×זר B vii 46–47, ידד B vii 48; מת ושר a binome? C 8. (cf. Sanch. Μουθ).

מת *husband, man* (H. pl. מְתִים, Akk. mutu): ימת מת || יאד אד C 40.

מתע: תמתע B ii 5.

מתק=מָתוֹק *sweet*: שפתם מתקתם *sweet lips* C 50, 55 (but adj. in dual!).

מתת: כמתת D v 17, see מות.

מת̄: ותלדן מת̄ D v 22.

מ×י *to come, go?* (cf. Aram. מטא, מטה, S. Arab. מטא?): A i 31, 32, ii 19, B ii 22, 23=iii 23 f., iv 31 f, v 106; מ×ני D vi 5, 8; תמ× D vi 28.

נ

נ *behold* (S. Arab. נ+אי Glaser 1606, l. 9; Eth. nâ; Heb. ־נָא): ון *and behold* B iv 50; ונאף B v 68.

נאי=נָאָה *to be pleasant*: Pi. ח̄מר ינאי *wine that gratifies* (cf. Ps. 104:15) C 6.

ני *pleasantness* (for form cf. רי <רוה Job 37:11, רית Mesha inscr.): לחם ני C 6.

נא̄ת *pleasantness, grace*: בנא̄ת אל T² 2:13.

נבט *to inspect* (H): Hif. לתבט B iii 21.

נבך: מבך נהרם *sources* (of rivers) (cf. מִבְכִי, with corrected vocalization מַבְכֵי, Job 28:11, and נִבְכֵי־יָם Job 38:16): A i 5, B iv 21.

נבלא *flame* (Akk. nablu, Eth. nabala): אשת ‖ נבלאת B vi 25 ff.

נבת=נֹפֶת *honey*: A iii 7, B i 32?, T 12:2.

נגח *to gore* (H): Nif. (reciprocal) ינגחן A vi 17.

נגש (=נָגַשׂ *to oppress?*): A ii 21, C 68.

נג̄ה: Impf. תנג̄ה A ii 6, 27.

נדד *to wander* (H): [—] עצר שמם ודג בים ונדד *the birds of the heavens and the fish in the sea and what wanders [in the earth?]* (of a bird Prov. 26:2; for phrase cf. Ps. 8:9) C 63.

נהד: אנהד D ii 22.

נהר = נָהָר *river*: pl. נהרם A i 5, B ii 7.

נוח *to rest* (H): אנחן A iii 18; juss. תנח A iii 19.

נוס *to flee* (H): juss. אל ינס B iii 5.

נחל: נחלת = נַחֲלָה *inheritance*: ארץ נחלתה *the land of his* (the god's) *inheritance* (cf. Ex. 15:17, Ps. 79:1) B viii 14, D ii 16.

נחת *to descend* (H): Pi. חטה נחת C 37; C 40; see מנן (cf. 2 Sam. 22:35).

נחל = נַחַל *valley, wady*: A iii 7.

נחת B i 34.

נטה: מט = מַטֶּה *staff*: מט ידה C 37, 40, 44.

נטט?: תטטן B vii 35.

ני see נאי.

נכל *Nikkal* (Bab. goddess Nin-gal, cf. Nerab inscr. l. 9): T 3:26.

נכת *to offer, sacrifice*?: דבחן נדבח || הו תע נתעי || הו נכת נכת T 2:24.

נסע *to remove* (H): juss. ליסע A vi 17.

נעל = נַעַל *sandal*?: B i 37.

נעם = נָעִים *gracious, good* (as in Phoen.): אלם נעמם C 1, 23, 58, 60. נעם = נֹעַם *favor*: נעם אלם *favor of the gods* D iii 15; לנעמי A ii 19 = D vi 6; fem. noun דבח נעמת (cf. Eze. 6:1[3]) C 27. נעמן = נַעֲמָן n. pr. T[5] 1 margin.

נפח: מפחם = מַפֻּחַ *bellows* B i 24.

נפי *to chase away, destroy*? (Arab. nafaya): נפינה B ii 5,7; T 2:20?

נפל *to fall* (H): D vi 8.

נפע: ינפע (cf. Arab.?) D iv 8.

נפר || עצרם A ii 22.

נפש = נֶפֶשׁ *soul, life, self*: A ii 17, 18, D i 7; נפש *my soul*, iii 19; בנפשה B vii 48; סלח נפש T 9:1; פנה ש נפש לבאת D i 14.

נץ = נֵץ *flower* (Gen. 40:11): T 12:5.

נצב *statue*? (cf. נְצִיב Gen. 19:26; Phoen. נצב): נצבת אל T² 1:7.

נקד *to bore*? (H): with suff. נקבנם B iv 11.

נקד: נקד = נֹקֵד *sheep-raiser*: relig. title? רב כהנם רב נקדם A sup. vi 55 (cf. Amos 1:1).

נקי *sheep* (Syr. naḳya): בחבר נקי, see חבר; misspelt variant נקנה B viii 19.

נקמד *Nḳmd*, king of Ugarit: B viii colophon; A sup. vi 56; see אגר; written Ni-iq-me-aš on an Akkadian tablet from Ras Shamra.

נקף: נקפת *turn of cycle* (cf. Is. 29.1, also תְּקוּפָה from rt. קוף): תמן נקפת C 67.

נר *Light* (H), deity: T 17: 10 (also in Sujin inscr. A a 9, after שמש). נרת: נרת אלם, epithet of שפש, A ii 24.

נש, pl. נשם *men* (cf. Syr. nāš): A ii 18; || אלם B vii 51.

נשא = נָשָׂא *to lift up*: תשא גה *she raised her voice?* A i 11 and passim; תשא אלאין בעל לכתך A sup. i 14; ישא יר שממה C 38 (cf. Dt. 4:19, 1 Sa. 17:20); juss. תשא D ii 16; impv. שא B viii 5?, pl. שא עדב C 54 || שא עדבתך (sing. required) C 65; inf. בנשא ענה *in the raising of his eyes* B ii 12.

נשק = נָשַׁק *to kiss*: C 51, 56.

נתן see יתן.

נחך = נָשַׁךְ *to bite*: Nif. (reciprocal) ינחכן A vi 19.

נחק B vii 39.

נ×ר: (= נָצַר *to watch*? Aram. נטר) נ×ר מדרע divine title: *Watcher of the Sown*? C 68, 69, 73; vocative י נ×ר נ×ר C 69–70 (for similar title, cf. Is. 27:2 f.); נ×ר B viii 14.

ס

סאן *shoe* (cf. סְאוֹן Is. 9.4, Akk. šēnu): A ii 10.

סבב = סָבַב *to change, exchange*: impf. נסב B vi 35; impv. סב B vi 34.

סבן D vi 3.

סכן: סכנת B i 43 (cf. שסכנמע B i 21?).

סלח = סָלַח *to pardon?*: סלח נפש T 9:1.

סמם = Aram. שמש Pael *to wait upon?*: ליסמסמת let them wait *upon Mot?* or *let M. attend?* B iv 15, or rt. יסם?

ספא: אספא D i 5.

ספר = סָפַר *to count*: יספר לחמש C 57; *to send?* תספר B viii 8 = D v 15.

ספר = סֵפֶר *document*: A sup. vi 53 (or *scribe*), T[2] 2:19. T[5] 1:1; ותבלם ספר? or מספר *account* B v 104.

סרך *to be associated* in לתסרך B v 66? but see יסר.

סתר *to hide* (H): Nif. יסתרן B vii 48.

ס̄

סס̄ו *horse* (cf. סוס): T[3] A 2, 4, 6, 10, B 17, 21, 32.

ע

עבד = עָבַד *to make*: ptcpl. פעבד אנך B iv 59–60; see פ.

עבד = עֶבֶד *slave*: עבדך אן D ii 12, 19.

עבדאלם n. pr. (= Phoen. עבדאלם): T[5] 1 margin.

עגל = עֵגֶל *calf*: עגלה A ii 28; pl. עגלם B vi 42; fem. עגלת D v 18.

עד = עַד *unto, until*: עד לחם B v 110 vi 55 עד אלם . . . תתלבן C 67; עד תשבע A sup. i 9.

עד = עַד *eternity*: ירחם על עד C 12 (cf. אֲבִי עַד Is. 9:5).

עד = עֵד *witness?*: עדך A sup. vi 47, 48.

עד: עדת B vii 16.

עדב = עָזַב (Neh. 3:8, cf. S. Arab. עדב) *to prepare, make*: A i 23, ii 22, juss. יעדבכם B viii 17; pass. B vi 39; עדב גפן אתנתה (?) B iv 7, 12; pass. תעדב כסא B v 108. With derivative nouns used of ritual offering: שא עדב לשפש C 54; שא עדבתך מדבר קדש C 65; הר עדב B vi 39 (cf. עזבנים Eze. 27:12); in a few cases the meaning of the root is not certain.

עדב = עָזַב *to leave alone?* perhaps in A i 23, ii 22, B viii 17.

עדד *to prepare* (Arab. ʻadda, IV): תעדדן D iv 25, Hitp. יתעדד רכב ערפת? B iii 11; noun || דלל B vii 46.

עדן Pi. *to make fruitful* and noun *fertility* (cf. עֵדֶן, Arab. ġaduna): B v 68–69.

עז = עַז *strong*: מת עז בעל עז A vi 17–20 (cf. בֹּעַז 1 Ki. 7:21, where B Βαλαζ, HP 55 Βooλαζ); עז מאד T² 2:13.

על = עַל *upon*: על אגן C 15; *over* ימלך על אלם B vii 49; *unto* על עד C 12; with suffixes עלך A v 11, עלם *to them?* T 5:9, עלנה *above him?* B iv 44 (cf. תַּחְתֵּנִי = Kalamû inscr. l. 14 תחתנה; for fem. נה– see עמנה under עם).

עלי = עָלָה *to go up*: juss. יעל A i 29, iv 5, D iv 20; pf. עלי B i 24; Shafel in perhaps cultic term תשעלינה בצררת צפ[ע]ן *she* (Anat) *shall raise* (?) *him* (the dead Aleyan) *to the heights of the North* A sup. i 15–16.

עלם = עוֹלָם *eternity*: חית עמעלם B iv 42 (cf. Gen. 3:22, etc.).

עלם = עֶלֶם *servant?* (Arab. ġlm): אחת אל ועלמה C 42, 49; בת אל ועלמה C 45–46; עבדך אן ודעלמך D ii 12, 19–20 (ד relative pronoun?).

עלן adverb *then?*: A vi 22, B i 38.

עם = עִם *with*, personally: A i 4, C 69, עמד D v 10, עמה A sup. i. 8, עמנה fem. D v 20; temporally עם עלם B iv 2 (cf. Ps. 72:5, Dan. 3:3); locally *at* B viii 2, 3, 4; עמי *to me*, *chez moi* T[2] 2:10, 19; לתתן פנם עם אל B iv 19, cf. A iv 31, B v 84, viii 1, D i 10, ii 14.

עם = עַם *people*: עממים *Peoples of the Sea?* B vii 55; cf. T[2] 1:3.

עמס *to load* (H): עמסמע A sup. i 12; יעמסנה || יכללנה B v 73?

עמק = עֵמֶק *valley*: A sup. i 5 = D vi 21.

עמר (= עֹמֶר?): יצק עמר אן לראשה עפר פלתת לקדקדה D vi 14–16.

ען = עַיִן *eye*: ענה *his eyes* B ii 12; *spring?* פל ענת שדם A iv 23 ff, ען A iv 42.

ען (?): ענאטענך D i 26.

עני = עָנָה *to answer*: pf. ען A ii 13, B vii 53; with suff. ענהם C 73; impf. ויען, ותען C i 19, 21; Hitp. יתען A v 16.

מען = מַעֲנֶה *answer*: מענך T[2] 2:15?, but see מען.

ענת *Anat*, goddess: בתלת ענת A ii 4; ע' אתר בעל A ii 30; B iv 18; T 3:16; ענתלתן T 9:17, see אל.

עפף: תעפף || תXצי B ii 10; see מגן.

עפר = עָפָר *dust*, *loose earth*: D vi 15, see עמר.

עץ = עֵץ *wood*, *tree*: with suff. עצה B vi 18; pl. עצם C 65; דם עצם B iv 38; פר עצם D ii 5–6.

עצר *bird* (Akk. iṣṣūru): ע' שמם C 62; C 38; pl. עצרם A ii 36, T 1:21.

עצר = מעצר *festival-place?* (cf. עֲצֶרֶת, and its observance in Baal's temple 2 Ki. 10:20): fragm to B vii.

עקל: עקלתן = עֲקַלָּתוֹן *tortuous*: D i 2, see לתן.

ער = עִיר *city*: B vii 9.

ער *to rouse, challenge?* (H) (cf. Job 3:8): יער מת בקלה A vi 31: Pa. תעררך B iv 39; impv. ערר B vii 7.

ער = עַיִר *young ass*: B iv 9, 14 (cf. Zec. 9:9).

ערב *to enter?* (Akk. erēbu): C 7, 12, 18, 62, 71, 74, D ii 3.

ערב = עֶרֶב *sunset*: ערב שפש T 9:9; C 74?

מערבי n. gent.: T^5 1:26, T^5 2:10.

ערב' *to pledge, exchange* (H): T 5:9.

ערף: ערפת *cloud* (Akk. urpāti): רכב ערפת *Rider of the Clouds* title of Aleyan Baal B iii 11, 18, v 122, D ii 7; תן קלה בע' B v 70; pl.(?) ערפתך D v 7 (see רח).

ערף: ערפת *hall* (=Phoen., cf. Arab. ġurfat): יפתח בדקת ע' B vii 19, 57 and fragm.

ערץ epithet of עתתר A i 26, 27.

עשר = עֶשֶׂר *ten*: ע' שקל T 5:12; עשר עשר (cf. Gen. 7:9, 15) T 5:2; *twelve* עשר תן [שקל] T 5:14; *fifteen* חמש עשרה T 1:10, *eighteen* תמנעשרה T^5 2:5; *twenty* עשרם T 5:9, תן לעשרם פאמת T 3:43.

עשבת || חרן: B v 76, 92, 99.

עתד: תעתד D iii 5.

עתן (or ענן) B viii 15.

עתק *to continue* (H) (cf. Job 21:7): ים ימם יעתקן A ii 5, 26.

עתתר *Athtar-Ashtar*, god: A i 26, 27.

עתתרת *Athtart-Ashtart*, goddess: בעל וע' T 9:8; ע' חר T 5:1 (see חר).

פ

פ *and* (so in Hadad inscr., =Arab. fa–): פעבד אנך B iv 59–60, D i 26 (?).

פ = פֹּה *here?*: T^2 2:12.

פ=פֶּה *mouth*: with suff. בפה B viii 18, D ii 4, בפי A ii 22, בפהם C 62, 64. See פה.

פאד place-name? if ד in דפאד is the relative particle (Arab. ḏû); see דפאד.

פאי A vi 11, 15.

פאם=פַּעַם, pl. *times*: פאמת שבע of choric repetition C 20; שלמם שבע פאמת T 5:7; ש' פאמת שבע T 3:52; חן לעשרם פאמת T 3:43. See also פען.

פאת=פֵּאָה: פאת מדבר *the direction* (*limit?*) *of the desert* (cf. לִפְאַת) C 68.

פגר *dawn* (=Arab. fajr): שפש פגר phase of deity T 1:12, 17 (cf. Mal. 3:20).

פד(י)=פָּדָה *to redeem?*: אפדך D i 5.

פדר *city* (Ḫaldian patari)?: || ער B vii 8, 10.

פדרי a deity (Anatolian Pitr?): B i 17, iv 55, T 1:15; בֹּעל בת פדרי T 14:3; פדרי בת אר D v 10.

פה *to speak?* (cf. Arab. fāha, denom. of fum): תפהן B ii 12; with suff. יפהנה B iv 27; פהת in parallel phrases A v 12–17=*I speak*, or a corresponding noun?

פוק: שפק *to offer* (Shaf. of פק or נפק): in cultic ceremony B vi 47–54; ופק B vi 56.

פחל *stallion* (=Arab.): צמד פ' B iv 5, 9; במת פ' B iv 15.

פחם=פֶּחָם *coal*: pl. || אשת B ii 9; C 41, 45, 48.

פחר divine *assembly* (Akk. puḫru): בתך פ[ח]ר בן אלם B iii 14 (cf. Ps. 82:1); פחר (cf. Dan. 8:11?) C 57; פחר בעל T 1:7; פחר אלם T 17:7.

מפחרת *assembly*: מ' בן [אל] T 2:17, 34 (cf. מ' אל גבל in Yeḥimilk inscr. from Byblos, פחר אל in S. Arab., and Is. 14:13).

פל *to fail, dry up?* (cf. Arab. falla): A iv 25, 26, 36, 37.

פלך = פֶּלֶךְ? *spindle* or *disk?* (Akk. pilakku): B ii 4.

פלסי n. pr. T[2] 2:2.

פלחֿת D vi 15, see עמר.

פן : פנם = פָּנִים *face*: A i 4 = B iv 20 = B v 84 = D i 10 = פן D ii 13; לפנם *before* (*them*)? B iv 17; פנה *his face* B v 108; פנך D v 12· פנה ש D i 14. פנשת D i 26.

פסל = פֶּסֶל *carved image?*: פסלחם ביער || ×ר באב D vi 17–18.

פען (formerly read צן) = פַּעַם *foot?*: פענה A iii 15, B iv 29; פענם B v 83; לפען A i 8, B iv 25, viii 26. See פאם.

פר : פרת = פָּרָה *cow*: D v 18.

פר = פְּרִי *fruit*: T[3] A obv. 11, B 15, D ii 5 (see יבל).

פרלן see אתן פרלן.

פרע : פרעת *long locks* (cf. פְּרָעוֹת Jud. 5:2): רמת פ׳ אבר B vii 56 and fragm. l. 9.

פרץ = פֶּרֶץ *breach*(?): C 70.

פרק *to unload?* (H): A iii 16.

פרש = פָּרַשׂ *to spread*: pass. ptcpl. פרשת בבר (so read for פרשא) B i 36.

פתח *to open* (H): יפתח B vii 17; ופתחהו (?) C 70.

פתי = פִּתָּה *to seduce*(?): אל אתֿתם כיפת C 39.

פחֿם B vi 13.

צ

צאן = צֹאן *sheep* (Akk. ṣēnu): B vi 41; תֿלתֿ צאן T 5:6; שבעם צאן A sup. i 22; מאד צאן D iii 22, 23.

צבא = צָבָא *host*: צבא שפש T 3:47, 53 (cf. Dt. 4:19).

צבט (H): מצבטם *tongs* (dual): B i 25.

צבע : אצבע = אֶצְבַּע *finger*: pl. with suff. אצבעתה B iv 30 (cf. Ex. 8:19).

צבר : צברת *company* (cf. צִבֻּר *heap* 2 Ki. 10:8, Mishn. Heb. צִבּוּר *congregation*): A i 12, B iv 47.

צוד *to hunt, roam?* (H): אצד A ii 15; תתלך ותצד D vi 25; תתלכן שד תצדן פאת מדבר C 68; for תצד C 16 see יצד(?).

צוח *to cry out* (H): יצח, תצח A i 11, 15, אצח D ii 21; *to summon*: pf. צח B vi 44.; impr. צח B v 75; perhaps ו(צ)חחם C 69.

צחא D i 22.

צחק *to laugh* (H): יצחק, of El, A iii 16 (cf. יִצְחָק and Ps. 37:13?); impr. f. B v 87.

צחר : צחררת *burning* (cf. Arab. ṣḥr): C 41; epithet of שפש A ii 24.

צחרמת A v 4.

צלל : מצלתם = מְצִלְתַּיִם *cymbals* reported in Syria xiv p. 141 (unpublished text).

צמד *harness* (cf. צֶמֶד): B iv 5, 9, T[2] 1:14; || כתף A v 3; verb, יצמדנן C 10.

צמק : צמקם = צִמּוּקִים *dry raisins*: T 12:57, T[3] A rev 2, B 34.

צע B i 42.

צפן = צָפוֹן *North*, the mount of El and the Elim: אלם בצפן B vii 6; צררת צפן A i 29, B v 117; אל צפן T 17:13; בעל צפן B vii 30, T 9:14; מרים צפן B iv 19, v 85, D i 11; as deity T 3:34, 9:7 (cf. בְּהַר מוֹעֵד בְּיַרְכְּתֵי צָפוֹן Is. 14:13; נְסִיכֵי צָפוֹן *princes of Saphon* Eze. 32:30 || *Sidonians*; the Egyptian sanctuary בַּעַל צָפוֹן). צררת צפען scribal error?, A sup. i 16.

צפען see צפן.

צרר : צררת *heights* (Arab. ṣirār, Akk. ṣirritu *district*): צ' צפן A i 29, B v 117, A sup. i 16.

צ̄

צ̄ל: צ̄ל כסף B ii 27.

צ̄לל: מצ̄לל *roof* (Aram. מטללא) or *roofed sanctuary* (cf. 2 Ki. 23:12, Jer. 19:13, and S. Arab. מט̄לל, see Rhodokanakis, *Studien* II 34): B i 13, 18, iv 52,56.

צ̄לם: בן צ̄למת רמת פרעת אֿבר B vii 55 and fragm. (cf. Akk. ṣalmat ḳaḳḳadi, *black of head*; here of עממים, the Peoples of the Sea?).

צ̄ר *upon* (Akk. ṣêr, Arab. ẓahr): B ii 20; בצ̄ר B i 35; לצ̄ר פחמם B ii 9, לצ̄ר קדקדה vii 4, לצ̄ר רחתם || על ידם B viii 6=D v 14.

ק

קבא *to speak* (Akk. ḳabū)?: קבאת A sup. vi 39.

קבלבל B i 37.

קבר *to bury* (H): Piel תקברנה A sup. i 17.

קבת A iv 42.

קדם=קֳדָם *in front of*: קדמה (or verb: *they presented him*) B v 107; קדם ידה B vii 40; קדמים B vii 34.

קדמן=קַדְמוֹן n. pr. *Cadmus*?: T5 1 margin.

קדקד=קָדְקֹד *skull*: B vii 4, D vi 16.

קדש=קָדוֹשׁ *holy*: קלה קדש B vii 29, 31; מדבר קדש C 65; קדשם || כהנם small tablet published at end of A sup. vi; name of a genius *Kadesh* paired with Amurru, see אמרר.

קול *to speak* (Arab. ḳāla): תקל A i 9, B iv 25; impr. קל B viii 27; קלת B iii 15? and A v 12?

קל=קול *voice*: תן קלה B v 70; בקלה A vi 32; B vii 29, 31; לתשת קל A sup. vi 41?

קום *to stand up* (H): יקם B iii 13; pf. קם quoted in Syria xiv p. 141 from an unpublished text.

קל *to be light* (H): A vi 21.

קלץ: יקלצן B iii 12.

קלקל=קְלֻקַל a plant? (Akk. ḳakḳullu): T³ A obv. 8.

קמח=קֶמַח *flour*: T³ A rev. 3.

קמץ (cf. Arab. rts. ḳamaṣa, ḳamaṭa?): B vi 43.

קן A sup. i 4=D vi 20.

קנא *to be jealous for?* (H): אקנא C 21; vii 1(?); perhaps in B v 81, 97, see אקנא.

קני *to possess* (H): ppl. f. קנית אלם *Mistress of the gods*, title of Athirat B i 23, iii 26, 30, iv 23 (cf. Gen. 14:19); קנין C 12?

קנץ *to conceive* (cf. כנס): Hitp. תקתנצן ותלדן C 58.

קץ=קֵץ *end*: A ii 11; אלקצם *to their end* B v 79.

קצב D ii 24.

קר: קרת=קֶרֶת *city* (cf. Phoen.): T 9:12; קרתה B viii 11, D ii 15; C 3 (or inf. of יקר?).

קרא *to call, invoke* (H): יקרא B vii 47, אקרא C 1, 23.

קרב *to approach* (H): juss. תקרב B vii 16; Shafel in cultic term שקרב *to sacrifice* (הִקְרִיב): תֹּר 'ש T 2:18.

קרב=קָרוֹב *near* A i 5; בקרב=בְּקֶרֶב *within* B v 76, vii 13, 27, D iii 19 (cf. בְּקִרְבָּם with Vss. at 2 Sam. 17:11).

קרד: אלאי קרדם D ii 10–11, 18 (=קַרְדֹּם *axe, battle-axe?*).

קרש *roof, abode* (cf. קֶרֶשׁ *deck* Eze. 27:6): of El A i 7.

ר

ראא: יראאן D ii 6 (perhaps form of rt. ראי?).

ראי=רָאָה *to see*: impf. יר C 38? but see יר; juss. f. תר B v 83?

ראת: ראת אל (written ראא) *a sight for El* B vi 42 (cf. רית לכמש, Mesha inscr. l. 12; and Ec. 5:10).

רְאֵם=ראם *wild ox* (Akk. rīmu): pl. A vi 18, B i 44, A sup. i 19, D i 17.

יאהף || כי יראש ססו :ראש of some equine malady (in the **head?**) T[3] A rev. 1 = B 21, 32.

רֹאשׁ=ראש *head, top*: ראשה A i 32, D vi 15, לראשהם C 5; pl. ראשם D i 3.

ירב :רב D ii 4.

רַב=רב :רבב *master*: רב כהנם T 18:1, A sup. vi 54–55 (= the Phoen. title), see also כהן; רבת *mistress*, title of goddesses רבת אתרת A i 16, רבת שפש C 54, רבת כמן B v 86, viii 25; רבם *great ones* A v 2?; fem. רבת D iii 2, 3.

רְבָבוֹת=רבבת *myriads*: B i 29, 44. See אלף.

בת רב = Akk. ēkallu, *great house, temple*: B i 18, iv 56, D v 11; see טלי.

אַרְבַּע=ארבע :רבע *four*: א' מתבת T 3:51; בארבע [עשרה] *on the fourteenth day* (see עשר) T 3:4; ארבע מאת T 12:1; רבעים *on the fourth day* (form = עָשׂוֹר Ex. 12:3) B vi 26.

רגם *to speak* (Akk. ragāmu): pf. D ii 8, לרגמת (with ל of asseveration?) B vii 23; juss. לירגם A v 7, ארגמך B i 21; impr. A iii 24, B viii 29, T 18:3 and T[2] 2:3 (introduction to a letter).

רגם *word*: C 52 (see יבל), T[2] 2:17; רגם יתּב T 3:45, 46; pl. B i 20.

רום *to be high* (H): impf. תרם C 32; ppl. pl. רמת *high* B vii 55 and fragm. l. 9; Polel רמם B v 114, תרממן B v 116; תרממת A sup. vi 43 (see צי×).

מרים *height* (=מָרוֹם: marwām>maryām, S. Arab. rt. רים, Eth. 'aryām, pl.): מרים צפן B v 85, D i 11 (cf. Is. 14:13).

רוּחַ=רח *wind*: (pl?) ואת קח ערפתך רחך מדלך מטרתך D v 7.

רח: du. רחם = רֵחַיִם *mill-stones*: A ii 34.

רחב (H): pl. רחבת ritual emblem of fem. organ || דכרנם D vi 53, (cf. הרחבת משכבך Is. 57:8); רחבת || ככנת A i 38?

רחד B iii 8.

רחם pl.(?) *affection* (רַחֲמִים): רחם ענת A ii 5, 27.

רחם n. pr. combined with אתרת as binome C 14, var. רחמי? C 16 (cf. Jud. 5:30).

רחת: רחתם B viii 6. = D v 14.

רכב (H.) ppl. *rider* or noun *construction* or the like; see ערף.

רפאם = רְפָאִים *the Shades*: רפאם תחתך A sup. vi 45, cf. Is. 14:9.

רפע: ליעדב מרח || לירפע עם *will rise up against* (cf. Arab.): A i 22–23.

רק *spices*? (Akk. riḳḳu): T 3:21.

רק *ingot*? (Akk. ruḳḳu): || לבנת B vi 34.

רשף *Reshef*, deity: T 1:7, 3:16, 17:5; בן רשף n. pr. (?) T⁵ 1:12.

רתק B vii 33.

ר×ב *to be hungry*? (H. רָעֵב): ר×ב ר×בת B iv 33, with inf. abs.

ר×ה: מר×תם in description of feast B iii 41, vi 56.

ש

ש = שֶׂה *sheep* (Kalummu inscr. ש, Sujin inscr. Ab 2, probably שאת, Akk. šu'u): T 1:2 and often as object of sacrifice, e. g. אלש בעלש דגנש T 9:3; פנה ש D i 14.

שא, see נשא.

שאל (H) *to ask*: שאל, שאלת T 18:9, 10 (fragm. of a letter) (for the form cf. שְׁאִלְתִּיו 1 Sam. 1:20).

שאר = שְׁאָר *remainder*: שארה A ii 25 (cf. Zeph. 1:4).

שב: שבת=שֵׂיבָה *gray hair*: B v 66.

שבני a gentilic?: A sup. vi 53.

שבע=שֶׁבַע *seven*: שבע פאמת C 20; שבע פאמת T 5:7, 3:52, 5:26; שבע לשבעם (=7+70?) D v 20; שבעת × למה C 20, cf. D v 8–9; שבעת ראשם D i 3; as ordinal=שָׁבוּעַ: בשבע ים *on the seventh day* B vi 32; C 66; שבעם *seventy* B vi 46; שבעני ול(ד) C 64? *sevenfold* (cf. שבענה Job 42:13) or goddess (cf. *Sibitti*, Amarna letters).

שבע *to satisfy* (H): [ע]דישב B vii 51?, עד תשבע A sup. i 9.

שבעד, see בעד.

שבר *Subaraeans?*: T 2:30.

שגר: . . . שגר מא D iii 16, 17.

שד=שָׂדֶה *open country*: A ii 20, 34, C 13, 68; באלף שד B v 86, 118, viii 25?

שדין A iv 42.

שדם: שדמת=שְׁדֵמָה *vine-plantation* C 10 (cf. Dt. 32:32 with play on סדם); שדם A ii 17, iv 25, 36, v 18?

שחוי *to bow down*: Hitp. impf. 2nd pers. f. תשתחוי A i 10, B viii 28.

שחלממת A ii 20.

שחר *Dawn*, a genius (cf. הילל בן שחר Is. 14:12, Phoen. nn. pr. שחרבעל, עבדשחר): שחר ושלם C 52, 53.

שים *to set* (H): תשם C 18; שמת C 21?

שיר *to sing* (H): ישר טב קל reported in Syria xiv p. 141 (unpublished text); שרה B v 71, see שר.

שית *to set* (H): impf. ישת C 39, ישתן B iv 14, כתשתה A sup. i 15, תשתנן *ib.* 17; juss. אשת B v 123, אל אשת D iii 11, אל תשת B v 126, with suff. אשתם B viii 15, ישתך A iv 26, 37?; impr. שת C 61, T[2] 2:18, T[3] A obv. 8, 10, B 8, 28; pf. pl. שת B v 107.

שכב *to lie down* (H): D v 19.

שכו *to mourn*? (Arab. šakā): Hitp. ישתך A iv 26.

שלח *to precipitate* a metal: ישלח || יצק B i 26. (for rt. cf. שִׁלֹחַ and Is. 8:6).

שלט: שליט *mighty*?: שליט ד שבעת ראשם D i 3.

שלם *to be safe* (H): ישלם, תשלם T 18:4, 5 and ישלם לך T² 2:4 (greetings in letters).

שלם = שֶׁלֶם *peace-offering*: pl. T 3:52, 57.

שלם *Salem*, deity (cf. Phoen. n. prr. שלמבעל, בתשלם יכנשלם): T 1:8, 3:17, 17:12; שחר ושלם C 52, 53; שלם C 7, 26?

שם = שֵׁם *name*?: pl. שמת C 21.

שמאל = שְׂמֹאל *left-hand*: אשמאל C 64.

שמח(?): שמחי D ii 25.

שמח = שָׂמֵחַ *to rejoice*: Pf. A iii 14, D ii 20; impr. f.? שמח B ii 28, v 82; Pi. תשמחה A i 11.

שמם = שָׁמַיִם *heavens*: A ii 25, B viii 23, C 38, 62; D i 4, ii 2; locative שממה C 38.

שמן = שֶׁמֶן *oil*: A iii 7, T 3:21, 44.

שמע *to hear* (H.): תשמע A sup. i 13; juss. ישמע B iv 8, אל ישמעך A vi 26, דתשמע T² 2:17; impr. m. and f. A i 16, iii 23; +iterative particle: שמע מע A vi 23, B vi 4; pf. שמעת T² 2:7.

שמר: שמרזת B i 33.

שן = שֵׁן *tooth*?: שן לכבכבם || שפת לשמם? D ii 3.

שנא: שנא הד *enemies of Haddu*? (cf. Ex. 20:5; etc.) B vii 36; B iii 17.

שנת = שָׁנָה *year*: בשבע שנת *in the seventh year* A v 9, C 66; pl. אב שנם (cf. עתיק יומין Dan. 7:9) A i 8; A v 8.

שסכן: +iterative particle שסכנמע B i 21.

שעל: משתעלתם or משקלתם (see under שקל).

שער: שערם = שְׂעֹרִים *barley*: T 12:1.

שפ: שפתם = שְׂפָתַיִם *lips*: שפתהם C 49, 50, 55; שת שפת לשמם *set a bound to heaven*? or *an incantation* (Akk. šiptu)? C 61, D ii 2.

שפי: שף *bare land* (שְׁפִי pl. שְׁפָיִם)?: pl. מדבר שפם C 4 (cf. Is. 41:18, Jer. 4:11, 12:12).

שפל *to fall* (H.): perhaps to be read for שה(?)ל C 32.

שפק see פוק.

שפש *Sun*, fem. deity (= שֶׁמֶשׁ, cf. שָׁבִים, Arab. subaisat): A vi 22, A sup. vi 44; usual title נרת אלם שפש A iv 32, iii 24 (where אל); שפש וירח T 5:11, 14; ערב שפש T 9:9; צבא שפש T 3:47, 53; שפש רבת C 54; T 1:12; C 25.

שצק see יצק.

שקל *to weigh* (H): *to raise up* (= Aram.) ישקל שדמתה כם גפן C 10, or = סָקַל *to remove stones* (cf. Is. 5:2); B vi 41?
שקל = שֶׁקֶל *shekel*: שקל חרץ T 5:10, 13; שקל כסף T 5:12, 15.
משקלתם du. *balances*? (if not to be read משתעלתם): C 31. 35–36.

שר = שַׂר *prince*: מת ושר C 7 (see מת); שר C 57?; שרם C 22?

שר: שרה || קלה B v 71 (cf. H. שִׁיר?).

שרין = שִׂרְיוֹן *Sirion* (Dt. 3:9, Ps. 29:6): B vi 19, 20.

שרף = שָׂרַף *to burn*: A ii 33.

שרף *burnt sacrifice* (Akk. šurpu): T 9:7; T² 1:16?

ששמן *sesame*: T 12:4.

ששר = שָׁשַׁר *vermilion* (Eze. 23:14): ארבע מתבת אזמר ששר בה T 3:51; D v 3?

שתי = שָׁתָה *to drink*: impf. A sup. i 10; לתשת . . . לתלחם A sup. vi 43; 1st pers. pl. תן ונשת C 72 (cf. Am. 4:1), with suff. אשתינה B iii 16; pf. 1st pers. שתת B iii 14, D i 25.

שתי *drink*, noun: שתי אלם B v 110, vi 55; שתי בחמר C 6.

ש̄

ש̄ד *breast* (= שַׁד, Arab. ṯady): ינקם באף ש̄ד C 61, supply in C 59 C 24 (where באפזד); perhaps ת̄ד in T 6:31.

ש̄ד: תגלי ש̄ד אל A i 6, B iv 23.

ש̄ר *vision?*: בחלם || בש̄רת A iii 5, 11.

ש̄רע: ש̄רעה A sup. i 4 = D vi 20.

ש̄רק: ש̄רקם D i 6.

ת

תבע *to follow?* (cf. Arab.); A iv 30, B iv 19, D i 9, ii 8, 13: see בעי.

תבח̄ח̄ B i 30.

תד B vi 32 (from rt. ידה?).

תהו = תֹהוּ *abyss*(?): D i 15.

תהם = תְהוֹם *the deep*: גף תהם C 30; du. תהמתם A i 6.

תחם *word, command* (cf. Aram.): T 18:3, T² 2:1, B viii 32, A iv 34, D i 12, ii 10; with suff. B iv 41; see הות.

תחת = תַּחַת *under*: fragm. l. 11 and B vii 57; תחתך A sup. vi 45, 46.

תטטן see נטט.

תטלי see טלי.

תך = תּוֹך *midst*: תך קרתה *in his city?* B viii 11, D ii 15; בתך צררת צפן B v 117; B viii 13; תך פנה *before him?* (cf. Zec. 13:6) B v 108.

תנן: בים ארש ותנן A sup. vi 50.

תצפן (or תפעפן) T 6:15.

ת×רך (rt. ×ר?) A iv 48.

תרף: תת̄כח תתרף D i 4.

תר×דס n. pr. T^2 2:5.

תר×זז place name (=Phoen. תרז Tarsus?): B viii 2.

תשע: תשעם = תִּשְׁעִים *ninety*: B vii 12.

תשרת month *Tishri*: ירח̄ ת' T 9:11.

ת̄

ת̄את *ewe* (Aram. תאתא): A ii 7, 29.

ת̄בר = שָׁבַר *to break*: A vi 29.

ת̄בר = Syr. noun tebārā with meaning of טֶרֶף *ravaging* (cf. Pesh. Nah. 3:1 למתבר תברא of the lion, Is. 5:29, Eze. 19:3): בת̄בר נקי *in the ravaging of the sheep* A ii 23; B viii 19.

ת̄ד = שָׁד *breast*, perhaps in T 6:31 (and cf. שד C 13?); but see ש̄ד.

. . . ת̄ד B vi 56.

ת̄דת: ת̄ת̄ = שֵׁשׁ *six* :B vii 9, T 12:1, 5, 11; pl. ת̄ת̄ם *sixty* ת̄ת לת̄ת̄ם B vii 9; ת̄[ד]ת̄ ים *on the sixth day* B vi 29.

ת̄וב = שׁוב *to do again, repeat*: impf. את̄בן אנך ואנחן (cf. Ps. 116:7) A iii 18, ית̄בן . . . יספר לח̣מש of ritual repetition? (see ת̄ני) C 56; impv. ת̄ב *return* B v 104, *again* B vii 8; Hif. תת̄ב *respond* B vi 2, B vii 24; Shaf.? רגם ית̄ת̄ב T 3:45.

ת̄כח: תת̄כח תתרף D i 4.

ת̄כל = שְׁכוֹל *infecundity*: || אלמן (cf. שְׁכוֹל וְאַלְמֹן Is. 47:9) C 8.

ת̄כף *to ruin* (Akk. sakāpu, šakāpu): Nif. pf. נת̄כף T^2 2:14.

ת̄כת B v 69.

תלחן = שֻׁלְחָן *table*: תלחן אל (cf. Mal. 1:7) B i 39; ends of all lines T 11; pl. תלחנת B iv 36; בתלחני *at my table*(*s*)? B iii 15

תלחני n. gent. T[5] 1:17.

תלת = שָׁלֹשׁ *three*: B iii 17, T 1:3, 5:6; תלתת T 5:5; pl. תלתם *thirty* T 1:20; תלת *third*? B vi 26.

תלת = שִׁלֵּשׁ *divide in three*?: A sup. i 5, D vi 20, 21.

תם = שָׁם *there* C 66.

תמת *there* T[2] 2:18.

תמם *there*? (cf. Syr. tammān): D iii 13, 27.

תמן = שְׁמֹנֶה *eight*: C 19, D v 9; תמנים *eighty* B vii 11; C 67; *eighteen* תמנעשרה T[5] 2:5; תמן לתמנים (see שבע) D v 21; בתמנת D iv 9?

תני = שָׁנָה Pi. *to repeat*: B vii 30; impr. תני || רגם B viii 31, D ii 9; תן לעשרם פאמת ritually T 3:43 (see תב), B vi 3. Hitp. ותתתני D iv 19?

תן = שֵׁנִי *second*: בים תן B ii 6, iii 16; ים ותן *a day and a second* (*day*) B vi 24.

תננם: ערבם ות' C 7, ערבם ת' C 26.

תעי *to offer up* and noun תע (cf. S. Arab.): A sup. vi 56 and colophon to B viii; דבחן נדבח || הו תע נתעי T 2:24.

תפד: יתפד A iii 15, B iv 29.

תפט = שָׁפַט *to judge* (S. Arab. תפט): תפטן *our judge* B iv 44.

מתפט = מִשְׁפָּט *judgment* A vi 29.

תק(?): תקנן or תתענן D ii 7.

תר = שׁוֹר *bull*: pl. תרם B vi 41; epithet of deities תר אל A iv 34, תרמן(?), תר מנם T 1:12, 15, see מן (cf. Ex. 32:4, 1 Ki. 12:28; also the divine title אביר ישראל; so frequently in S. Arab. Bull, a divine title, e. g. Taur Ba'al)..

ת̄רמג place name: B viii 3 (cf. Gen. 10:3?).

ת̄רמן place name: A sup. vi 57.

ת̄ת̄ see ת̄דת̄.

×

×אף: מ×אפת C 75.

×די: ב×דין אל T^2 1:18.

×זר place-name *Zinzar*? (Amarna, no. 30, Egyptian *Senzar*, modern *Sheizar* in Orontes valley): ידד אל ×זר A vi 31, B vii 47, viii 32; ×צר ארץ B viii 4; שבעד ×זרם C 14, תחגרן ×זר C 17.

×לם: שבעת ×למה A vi 8; שבעת ×למה ת̄מן ח̄נזרך D v 8–10; ל×למה B ii 29; תלאכן ×למם B v 105; ל×למה B vii 52; ב×למת עממים B vii 55.

×מא: = צָמֵא *to be thirsty*: ×מא ×מאת B iv 34.

×נב C 26.

×צי: מגן || מ×צ̄ B i 23; תעפף || ת×צ̄י B ii 11; ת×צ̄ין B iii 26, 29; מגנתם || ×צ̄תם B iii 31, cf. also B iii 35; ת×צ̄ית A sup. vi 44 (see רום); מ×צ̄י D v 24–25.

×ר *mountain* (צור, Aram. טור)?: || גבע A ii 16; B vii 5, 37; ×ר תר×זז B viii 2, ×ר ת̄רמג viii 3; ×ר כנכני D v 12–13; שא ×ר על ידם B viii 5, D v 13; pl. גבעם || ×רם B v 77, 93; vii 32.

×ר: פסלתם ביער || ×ר באבן (cf. צִיר *idol?*): A sup. i 2 = D vi 17; perhaps here ×ר of B viii 5, D v 13 above.

SUPPLEMENT

As noted in Postscript to the Preface, we here present, without further commentation, the fresh text edited by M. Virolleaud in the current volume of *Syria*, pp. 29–45, under the title, "La révolte de Košer contre Baal: Poème de Ras-Shamra." The one other treatment of this text, so far as known, will appear in *Journ. Am. Or. Soc.*, 1935, part 3, under the title "Ras Shamra Notes IV: The Conflict of Baal and the Waters," by J. A. Montgomery. As these titles indicate, the two treatments take contradictory positions on the myth involved. We add also a Vocabulary of fresh words in this text, supplemental to the Glossary above.

E

. . . . י* . . . תת | מתת . . .
. . . . . חי . . . . לאשצא | הם | אף | אמר . . .
. . . . ובים | מנח לאבד | בים | ארתם | מ . . .
. . . | נהר | תלעם | תם חרבם | אתס | אנשק
. התם | לארץ | יפל | דלני | ול | עפר | עצם | אי
(ב)פה | רגם | ליצא | בשפתה | הותה | ותתן | גה יא×ר
תחת כסא | זבל ים וען | כתר וחסס לרגמת
לך | לזבל | בעל | תנת | לרכב | ערפת | הת | אבך
בעלם | הת | אבך | תמחץ | הת | תצמת צרתך
תקח | מלך | עלמך | דרכת דת דר דרך
כתר צמדם | ינחת | ויפער | שמתהם | שמך את
יגרש | יגרש | גרש ים | גרש ים לכסאה

l. 1: After י comes נ or ר then a badly broken letter followed by י or ח.

נִהר לכחתֿ דרכתה | תרתקץ בד בעל כם נֹש
ר באֿצבעתה | הלם | כתףּ זבל | ים | בן | ידם
(תֿפֿ)ט נהר | ירתקץ | צמד | בד בעל | כם | נשר
בְּ(אֿ)צבעתה | ילם | כתף | זבל ים | בן ידם | תֿפט
נהר עז | ים לימך | לתנ×צן | פנתה | לידלףּ
תמנה | כתֿר צמדם ינחת | ויפער | שמתהם
שמך | את | אימר | אימר | מר ים | מר ים
לכסאֿה | נהר לכחתֿ | דרכתה | תרתקץ
בד בעל | כם | נשר באֿצבעתה | הלם | קדק
ד זבל ים | בן | ענם | תֿפט | נהר | יפְרסח ים
ויקל | לארץ | וירתקץ | צמד בד בעל
כְ(ם) נשר | באֿצבעתה | ילם | קדקד | זבל
(ים) בן | ענֻם | תֿפט | נהר | יפרסח | ים | יקל
לארץ | תנ×צן | פנתה | וידלףּ | תמנה
יקתֿ בעל | וישת | ים | יכלי תֿפט | נהר
בשם | תגערם | עתֿתרת | בתֿ לאלאֿין ב(על)
בתֿ | לרכב | ערפת | כשבין | זב(ל ים)
שבין | תֿפט | נהר | ויצא ב ...
יבתֿ | נן | אלאֿין | בעל | ו ...
ים | למת | בעלם ים ל ...
חם | לשרר | ו ...
יען | ים | למת | ...
לשרר | ותע...
בעלם | המת ...
לשרר | ש ...
בראֿשה | ...
. בה* | מש ...
. ן | ענה ...

l. 39: First letter י or חֿ.

אבד = H. *to wander.*

אי divine name = (?), cf. אימר.

אימר divine name.

אמר *to speak, command* (? = H.).

ארתם.

את || חרב, a weapon, cf. אֵת 2 Ki. 6:5.

אתם verbal part.

בד *community* (= Phoen. bod).

בות = בוש, Hif. יבת נן 'shames me.' בת *shame.*

בן = בֵּין *between.*

גרש = H. *to storm*, of waters (cf. Is. 57:20).

דלן noun from *dll* = זָלַל *to despise?*

דלף verb.

הת *behold?*

יצא = H. *to go out.*

לם? *to strike* (cf. הָלַם), Hif. הלם, impf. ילם.

מר *lord* (= Phoen. element?), or verbal?

נהר deified *River.*

נוח : מנח = מָנוֹחַ *resting-place* (?).

נשק : אנשק verbal part.

נשר = נֶשֶׁר *eagle.*

נשת = H. *to dry up* (for phrase cf. Is. 19:5).

נ×ץ verb.

עצם = עָצַם *to be strong*, ppl.

פנת *surface* (cf. Syr. panthā, J. Aram. 'appantā)?

פער : *to scold* (cf. Arab.)?

פרסח *to suppress* (= Akk. pulasuḫu).

צאב verb.

צמד : *band, congregation?* || צמד בד (cf. Syr.). In divine epithet כתר צמדם.

צמת = H. *to destroy.*

צרת = צָרָה, abstract for *enemies* (cf. אֵיבָתִי Mic. 7:8).

קלל : יקל = Hif., *to make light, raise?*

קת = rt. קית (Arab.) *to collect.*

רקץ: *to move, dance* (=Arab. rḳṣ, Aram. rḳd).

שם = שֵׁם name, pl. שמת.

שצא *to deliver* (Akk. ušēṣi, B.. Aram. שיציא), or *to destroy* (Targ. שיצי).

שרר.

תלע.

תמן = Akk. tēmennu, *foundation?*

אר verb.

P. S. M. Dussaud has published a full treatment of this text in current Part of *Syria*, pp. 196–204, "Les éléments déchainés".

www.ingramcontent.com/pod-product-compliance
Lightning Source LLC
LaVergne TN
LVHW020636100826
845148LV00012B/2201

* 9 7 8 1 6 0 6 0 8 3 7 8 9 *